CUSTOM CURRICU[LUM]

In the Beginning... What?

Paul
Borthwick

Pam
Campbell

Cook Ministry Resources
a division of Cook Communications Ministries
Colorado Springs, Colorado/Paris, Ontario

Custom Curriculum
In the Beginning . . . What?

© 1994 David C. Cook Publishing Co.

All rights reserved. Except for the reproducible student sheets, which may be copied for ministry use, no part of this book may be reproduced in any form without the written permission of the publisher, unless otherwise noted in the text.

Unless otherwise noted, Scripture quotations are from the Holy Bible, New International Version (NIV), © 1973, 1978, 1984 by International Bible Society. Used by permission of Zondervan Bible Publishers.

Cook Ministry Resources
a division of Cook Communications Ministries
4050 Lee Vance View, Colorado Springs, CO 80918-7100
Cable address: DCCOOK
Series creator: John Duckworth
Series editor: Randy Southern
Editor: Randy Southern
Option writers: Stan Campbell, John Duckworth, Sue Reck, and Randy Southern
Designer: Bill Paetzold
Cover illustrator: Dan Hobbs
Inside illustrator: Joe Weissmann
Printed in U.S.A.

ISBN: 0-7814-5164-7

CONTENTS

About the Authors — 4

You've Made the Right Choice! — 5

Creation and World Views
by Paul Borthwick — 9

Publicity Clip Art — 14

Sessions by Pam Campbell
Options by Stan Campbell, John Duckworth, Sue Reck, and Randy Southern

Session One
The Creation of Order — 16

Session Two
The Creation of Man and Woman — 32

Session Three
The Creation of Rest and Worship — 44

Session Four
The Creation of a New Plan — 58

Session Five
The New Creation — 74

About the Authors

Pam Campbell is a writer, editor, and church youth director living in Woodridge, Illinois. A youth worker for almost twenty years, she has written several books including the BibleLog series for adults (Victor).

Stan Campbell has been a youth worker for almost twenty years and has written several books on youth ministry including the BibleLog series (SonPower) and the Quick Studies series (David C. Cook). Among the books he's written in the Custom Curriculum series are *Hormone Helper, Just Look at You!, What Would Jesus Do?* and *Your Bible's Alive!* Stan and his wife, Pam, are youth directors at Lisle Bible Church in Lisle, Illinois.

John Duckworth is a writer and illustrator in Carol Stream, Illinois. He has worked with teenagers in youth groups and Sunday school, written several books including *The School Zone* (SonPower) and *Face to Face with Jesus* (in the Custom Curriculum series), and created such youth resources as Hot Topics Youth Electives and Snap Sessions for David C. Cook.

Sue Reck is an editor for Chariot Family Products. She is also a freelance curriculum writer. She has worked with young people in Sunday school classes, youth groups, and camp settings.

Randy Southern is a product developer of youth material at David C. Cook and the series editor of Custom Curriculum. He has also worked on such products as Quick Studies, Incredible Meeting Makers, Snap Sessions, First Aid for Youth Groups, Junior Highs Only, and Pathfinder Electives.

You've Made the Right Choice!

Thanks for choosing **Custom Curriculum!** We think your choice says at least three things about you:

(1) You know your group pretty well, and want your program to fit that group like a glove;

(2) You like having options instead of being boxed in by some far-off curriculum editor;

(3) You have a small mole on your left forearm, exactly two inches below the elbow.

OK, so we were wrong about the mole. But if you like having choices that help you tailor meetings to fit your kids, **Custom Curriculum** *is* the best place to be.

Going through Customs

In this (and every) **Custom Curriculum** volume, you'll find
- five great sessions you can use anytime, in any order.
- reproducible student handouts, at least one per session.
- a truckload of options for adapting the sessions to your group (more about that in a minute).
- a helpful get-you-ready article by a youth expert.
- clip art for making posters, fliers, and other kinds of publicity to get kids to your meetings.

Each **Custom Curriculum** session has three to six steps. No matter how many steps a session has, it's designed to achieve these goals:

• *Getting together.* Using an icebreaker activity, you'll help kids to be glad they came to the meeting.

• *Getting thirsty.* Why should kids care about your topic? Why should they care what the Bible has to say about it? You'll want to take a few minutes to earn their interest before you start pouring the "living water."

• *Getting the Word.* By exploring and discussing carefully selected passages, you'll find out what God has to say.

• *Getting the point.* Here's where you'll help kids make the leap from principles to nitty-gritty situations they are likely to face.

• *Getting personal.* What should each group member do as a result of this session? You'll help each person find a specific "next step" response that works for him or her.

Each session is written to last 45 to 60 minutes. But what if you have less time—or more? No problem! **Custom Curriculum** is all about . . . options!

What Are My Options?

Every **Custom Curriculum** session gives you fourteen kinds of options:

• *Extra Action*—for groups that learn better when they're physically moving (instead of just reading, writing, and discussing).

• *Combined Junior High/High School*—to use when you're mixing age levels, and an activity or case study would be too "young" or "old" for part of the group.

• *Small Group*—for adapting activities that would be tough with groups of fewer than eight kids.

• *Large Group*—to alter steps for groups of more than twenty kids.

• *Urban*—for fitting sessions to urban facilities and multiethnic (especially African-American) concerns.

• *Heard It All Before*—for fresh approaches that get past the defenses of kids who are jaded by years in church.

• *Little Bible Background*—to use when most of your kids are strangers to the Bible, or haven't made a Christian commitment.

• *Mostly Guys*—to focus on guys' interests and to substitute activities they might be more enthused about.

• *Mostly Girls*—to address girls' concerns and to substitute activities they might prefer.

• *Extra Fun*—for longer, more "rowdy" youth meetings where the emphasis is on fun.

• *Short Meeting Time*—tips for condensing the session to 30 minutes or so.

• *Fellowship & Worship*—for building deeper relationships or enabling kids to praise God together.

• *Media*—to spice up meetings with video, music, or other popular media.

• *Sixth Grade*—appearing only in junior high/middle school volumes, this option helps you change steps that sixth graders might find hard to understand or relate to.

• *Extra Challenge*—appearing only in high school volumes, this option lets you crank up the voltage for kids who are ready for more Scripture or more demanding personal application.

Each kind of option is offered at least twice in each session. So in this book, you get *almost 150* ways to tweak the meetings to fit your group!

Customizing a Session

All right, you may be thinking. *With all of these options flying around, how do I put a session together? I don't have a lot of time, you know.*

We know! That's why we've made **Custom Curriculum** as easy to follow as possible. Let's take a look at how you might prepare an actual meeting. You can do that in four easy steps:

(1) *Read the basic session plan.* Start by choosing one or more of the goals listed at the beginning of the session. You have three to pick from: a goal that emphasizes *knowledge,* one that stresses *understanding,* and one that emphasizes *action.* Choose one or more, depending on what *you* want to accomplish. Then read the basic plan to see what will work for you and what might not.

(2) *Choose your options.* You don't *have* to use any options at all; the

basic session plan would work well for many groups, and you may want to stick with it if you have absolutely no time to consider options. But if you want a more perfect fit, check out your choices.

As you read the basic session plan, you'll see small symbols in the margin. Each symbol stands for a different kind of option. When you see a symbol, it means that kind of option is offered for that step. Turn to the options section (which can be found immediately following the Repro Resources for each session), look for the category indicated by the symbol, and you'll see that option explained.

Let's say you have a small group, mostly guys who get bored if they don't keep moving. You'll want to keep an eye out for three kinds of options: Small Group, Mostly Guys, and Extra Action. As you read the basic session, you might spot symbols that tell you there are Small Group options for Step 1 and Step 3—maybe a different way to play a game so that you don't need big teams, and a way to cover several Bible passages when just a few kids are looking them up. Then you see symbols telling you that there are Mostly Guys options for Step 2 and Step 4—perhaps a substitute activity that doesn't require too much self-disclosure, and a case study guys will relate to. Finally you see symbols indicating Extra Action options for Step 2 and Step 3—maybe an active way to get kids' opinions instead of handing out a survey, and a way to act out some verses instead of just looking them up.

After reading the options, you might decide to use four of them. You base your choices on your personal tastes and the traits of your group that you think are most important right now. **Custom Curriculum** offers you more options than you'll need, so you can pick your current favorites and plug others into future meetings if you like.

(3) *Use the checklist.* Once you've picked your options, keep track of them with the simple checklist that appears at the end of each option section (just before the start of the next session plan). This little form gives you a place to write down the materials you'll need, too—since they depend on the options you've chosen.

(4) *Get your stuff together.* Gather your materials; photocopy any Repro Resources (reproducible student sheets) you've decided to use. And . . . you're ready!

The Custom Curriculum Challenge

Your kids are fortunate to have you as their leader. You see them not as a bunch of generic teenagers, but as real, live, unique kids. You care whether you really connect with them. That's why you're willing to take a few extra minutes to tailor your meetings to fit.

It's a challenge to work with real, live kids, isn't it? We think you deserve a standing ovation for taking that challenge. And we pray that **Custom Curriculum** helps you shape sessions that shape lives for Jesus Christ and His kingdom.

—***The Editors***

Creation and World Views
by Paul Borthwick

Is my faith relevant to the world? How does being a Christian affect the way I look at science or the physical universe? What impact does my faith have in understanding or responding to the interpersonal problems in our world—from family breakdown to war?

Most junior highers do not actively wrestle with these deep issues, at least on a conscious, daily basis. In the church, those who contemplate such questions often develop an unhealthy "dualism"—a separation between the spiritual and the real issues of daily living. These kids see (often as a result of watching older Christians) building a relationship with God and understanding science on two different, never-connecting planes.

During early adolescence, young people form their opinions as to whether or not their faith has any *real* relevance to the world. In these developing years, kids make one of three decisions:

(1) to develop a faith which is spiritual only, unrelated to the physical world in which we live;

(2) to abandon their faith in favor of "real life" issues;

(3) to integrate faith with the entirety of life.

The third option is our choice.

In the sessions that follow, you will lead group members in discussions and questions in hopes of instilling an integration of faith and world view. Your goal is to help group members understand that their Christian faith is not only life-changing on the spiritual level, but also relevant and important to answer questions like "Where did we come from?" and "Why is there evil in the world?"

Remember the World from Which Your Kids Come

A veteran youth worker recently gave me this advice: "When preparing to address today's young people, *don't assume that they know anything in the spiritual/biblical arena.*" Tough words, but very true with many of the young people coming our way. Even kids from Christian homes often lack basic Bible knowledge.

This biblical illiteracy affects the way kids approach topics. Their assumptions might not be ours. Our beliefs may conflict with theirs. Before launching into these studies related to origins, consider the formative factors influencing most of your group members' world views. [NOTE: Kids coming from Christian schools or home schooling settings could be markedly different, but these factors definitely affect public school-educated and media-influenced youth.]

Kids come from a *secularistic* world. Many students in public schools have been taught evolution as fact, not as one theory among many. As a result, the biblical creation account may sound like science fiction to them. The themes that you introduce in the weeks ahead may be radically different than what they have learned thus far. You need to brace yourself for all sorts of questions from those who approach creation or the problem of sin from a secular vantage point.

Kids come from a *humanistic* world. Introduce the topic of original sin, and some group members may cry "foul." They believe that humankind is basically good. Many have been taught that humanity needs only a little social or behavioral engineering to discover the basic goodness within. Identifying the sin problem as the core of evil and calling humanity "fallen" may deeply challenge your group members (and, in some cases, their humanistic parents).

Kids come from a *pluralistic* world. In this world, all beliefs have equal value, and no one has a grasp of absolute truth. This is what kids learn from secular society. As a result, introducing the Judeo-Christian God as the starter of the world and Master of the Universe will contradict the "Everybody's OK no matter what they believe" spirit of the age.

Kids come from an *environmentally aware* world. This is potentially good news. Stewardship of the earth may be easier to teach because more people are thinking of saving the earth—but it also has its challenges. This book teaches stewardship based on a God-ordained responsibility ("dominion") given to humanity. Contrary to popular views, the earth is not our mother and apes are not our forefathers.

Prepare Yourself for Action

The topics in this book require some preparation, so to lead these sessions effectively, consider the following steps:

• *Research.* What are your group members learning at school? What is the world view that they bring to the discussions? An interview with a biology or sociology teacher at a local public school can tell you what is being taught regarding Creation or the problem of evil in the world. Interview a few students—some from within the youth group and others who are not church-goers—to find out what they really believe about issues like evolution, ecology, or sin in the world. Are the Christian students' beliefs any different than the non-Christians'?

Understanding what students are learning at school and what they really believe may prepare you for some of their questions. It will also help you direct them from where they are to where you want them to be biblically.

• *Look for supplemental help.* Do you know of any Christians who teach science or biology who could address your group members to introduce some of the topics? What video resources can you draw on? Can the Creation Institute assist you with materials on scientific creationism? No one expects you to be an expert scientist, but you can enhance the sessions greatly by calling on some outside experts for their help.

• *Review Scripture.* Whenever the discussion turns to controversial issues like evolution or ecology, I am tempted to discuss my opinions rather than what the Bible teaches. Researching relevant Scripture passages helps us remember not only what the Bible teaches, but also what the Bible does *not* teach.

Prepare for questions in the weeks ahead on issues like the age of the earth, the evident goodness in human societies who have never heard of Jesus Christ, or the dilemma of Jesus being with God and being God at the same time. Where Scripture teaches clearly, be firm; but when Scripture is either unclear or silent, exercise freedom to allow for a range of opinions. For example, we emphasize the fact that God creates, that He is the ultimate starting point. Whether or not He created everything in seven twenty-four-hour time periods is open to wide discussion.

Lead by Example

In the weeks ahead, the best way to excite group members is to get thoroughly involved in the topics. We lead by example by wrestling with *real* questions: Why does God allow evil? What is my responsibility in the management of the environment? How can Jesus and God *both* be the Creator?

We lead by example by allowing for disagreement. In attempting to teach group members an integrated faith and world view, we can try to create an environment where every question is considered legitimate. If we laugh off questions that we deem silly or scoff at questions that are clearly unbiblical, kids will leave our meetings thinking, *I have these questions, but they are obviously not allowed in the religious context.* Through our responses, we force the dualism we are trying to avoid.

We lead by example by keeping topics in proportion to the most important doctrine: salvation. Belief in some version of creation is *not* required for salvation. Maintaining specific convictions about the stewardship of the earth does not forgive sins. People find salvation through trust in Jesus Christ, not based on whether or not they adhere to a particular view on the origins of humanity. Session 4 especially emphasizes that our goal is to show kids how to be restored to a right relationship with God, not to refute the theories of Charles Darwin.

Finally, we lead by example by implementing what we learn together. A youth group clean-up day could be the response to a discussion of "dominion" over the earth. A discussion of how Jesus' redemption affects our view of fallen humanity can illustrate to kids how a sinful nature in human beings should not keep us from reaching out in love. Perhaps we could organize a walk in some beautiful natural setting with a concentrated time of thanking God and Jesus for the magnificence of creation. Implementation helps group members answer the question "What difference does it make?" by giving them practical responses to these biblical truths.

Our goal? To help young men and women begin to wrestle with a world view that integrates their lessons in biology class with their understanding of who God is. We want to produce young people who see their faith as relevant and essential for addressing the real problems and issues in our world. The sessions ahead serve that equipping process.

Paul Borthwick is minister of missions at Grace Chapel in Lexington, Massachusetts. A former youth pastor and frequent speaker to youth workers, he is author of several books including Organizing Your Youth Ministry *and* Feeding Your Forgotten Soul: Spiritual Growth for Youth Workers *(Zondervan).*

Publicity Clip Art

The images on these two pages are designed to help you promote this course within your church and community. Feel free to photocopy anything here and adapt it to fit your publicity needs. The stuff on this page could be used as a flier that you send or hand out to kids—or as a bulletin insert. The stuff on the next page could be used to add visual interest to newsletters, calendars, bulletin boards, or other promotions. Be creative and have fun!

Specially Designed by God

If you think God's work in the world stopped after He made Adam and Eve, have we got a surprise for you! Join us as we take a fresh and exciting look at creation—and what it means to us today—in a new series called *In the Beginning . . . What?*

Who:

When:

Where:

Questions? Call:

In the Beginning . . . What?

In the Beginning . . . What?

He's still got the whole world in His hands.

Tell your friends.

(Fill in the speech balloon with your own words.)

You'll be upset if you miss this meeting.

SESSION 1

The Creation of Order

YOUR GOALS FOR THIS SESSION:
Choose one or more

☐ To help kids see how God personally created order from chaos at the beginning of the world.

☐ To help kids understand how God's creativity is reflected and sustained by Him in all aspects of His creation.

☐ To helps kids consider how God can personally create something out of seemingly confused, empty lives.

☐ Other _____

Your Bible Base:

Genesis 1:1-31
Job 33:4

C U S T O M   C U R R I C U L U M

Ankle-Deep in Chaos

(Needed: Multi-colored pairs of socks, blindfolds, three laundry baskets)

As kids arrive, have them form pairs. Give each pair a blindfold. For each pair of group members, you'll need to have at least one pair of matching socks. Put all of the socks in three laundry baskets. Have the members of each pair decide who will be the "sock director" and who will be the "sock hunter." The sock hunter must wear the blindfold. Explain that at your signal, the blindfolded kids must find their way to one of the laundry baskets and begin trying on socks until they find a matching pair. The sock directors will try to guide their sock hunters to one or more of the baskets to find a matching pair of socks. However, the sock directors may use only the following words in giving directions: *right, left, forward, back, yes, no.* Award two pairs of socks to the first pair that finds a matching set of socks. In addition, you may want to award a pair of socks to the person who tries on the most socks before finding a match.

Udder Chaos

(Needed: Cut-apart copies of Repro Resource 1, copies of Repro Resource 2, pencils, colored markers)

Distribute a cut-apart copy of "Udder Chaos" (Repro Resource 1) to each group member. Give kids a few minutes to put the puzzle together. After everyone has completed the puzzle, ask: **How would you define the word *chaos*?** If no one mentions it, suggest that *chaos* is usually considered a state of "udder" confusion.

Ask: **What does it feel like to be in a state of utter confusion? When was the last time you experienced chaos?** Get several responses.

Hand out copies of "Wheel of Life" (Repro Resource 2), pencils, and

17

colored markers. Give the following instructions: **Label the various areas or activities of your life according to the amount of time you spend in each. For example, you might allow 8-10 hours for sleeping, 1-2 hours for meals, etc. Then use the colored markers to reflect the areas of your life that seem snarled, confused, cluttered, or chaotic. You might want to use "warm" colors—reds, oranges, and yellows—to indicate severe chaos and "cool" colors—blues, greens, and purples—to indicate areas that seem normal, orderly, or peaceful.**

After a few minutes, have group members share their color wheels, explaining why some areas or activities in their lives seem chaotic. Be sure to note the stressors in your kids' lives as group members explain their sheets. This will help you guide the discussions later in the session and will make you more sensitive to your kids' needs.

STEP 3

Out of Nowhere

(Needed: Bibles, poster board, colored markers)

Have kids form teams. Distribute poster board and colored markers to each team. Assign one or more of the following passages to each team:
- Genesis 1:3-5
- Genesis 1:6-8
- Genesis 1:9-13
- Genesis 1:14-19
- Genesis 1:20-23
- Genesis 1:24-31

Instruct each team to read its assigned passage(s) and then illustrate as much as possible what God created on that day. On the back of the poster board, the team should write the corresponding day of creation.

After a few minutes, reassemble the group, collect the posters, and ask for a volunteer. Instruct the volunteer to arrange the posters in order according to the day of creation. (Of course, the volunteer may not look at the back of the posters.) Once the volunteer gets the days in order, display the posters around the room.

Have someone read aloud Genesis 1:1, 2. Then ask: **What do these two verses tell us about the Creator of the universe? What difference does it make whether the universe origi-**

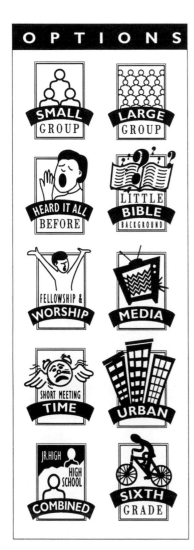

nated from a living God or from lifeless matter?

If you lived in a universe that was cold, lifeless, or dead, how would you feel about yourself, your future, and what's important in life?

Get several responses to these questions. Then point out that these verses, as well as the remainder of Genesis 1, affirm that God designed and created our world. The objects that fill our world were created by God as well. Explain that in this session you will not concern yourself with *how* the universe was created; rather, you will focus on the fact that everything around us has been carefully and thoughtfully designed.

Draw kids' attention to the words *formless* and *empty* in Genesis 1:2. Explain: **God alone can bring form out of formlessness and fullness out of emptiness. Let's take a look at the first three days of creation and see how He brought form or structure to the universe.**

Have someone read aloud Genesis 1:3-5. Then ask: **What form or structure did God design on the first day?** (He created light and separated light from darkness.)

How did God begin the act of creation? (By speaking.)

What did He think about His creation? (He saw it was good.)

Notice that God spoke His creation into existence, naming each part. Why do you think God referred to the light as "good"? Why didn't He refer to the darkness as "good"? Get opinions from several group members.

Have someone read aloud Genesis 1:6-8. Then ask: **What form or structure did God create on the second day?** (He created an expanse to separate the water above from the water below.)

What part of creation did God name on the second day? (The sky.)

Have someone read aloud Genesis 1:9-13. Then ask: **What form or structure did God design on the third day?** (He separated the land from the seas.)

On the third day, God began to fill the emptiness of His creation. What did He fill the earth with? (Vegetation—plants and trees.)

Have someone read aloud Genesis 1:14-19. Then say: **God continued to furnish His creation on the fourth day. What did He create to fill the atmosphere or sky that He'd created on the second day?** (The sun and moon.)

Describe the functions of the heavenly bodies created by God. (The sun was to govern the day and the moon was to govern the night.)

Have someone read aloud Genesis 1:20-23. Then ask: **How did God continue to furnish His creation—specifically, the seas and the air—on the fifth day?** (He created fish and birds to inhabit the seas and the sky.)

Describe the responsibilities of the living things created by God on this day. (They were to mutliply and increase in number to fill the seas and the air.)

Have someone read aloud Genesis 1:24-31. Then ask: **How did God complete His work on the sixth day?** (He made land creatures—including humans.)

What was unique about the way God created humans, compared with the rest of His creation? (Humans were created in God's image.)

What clues do you have that people—men and women—are special creations of God? (In addition to being created in God's image, humans were given dominion over the rest of creation.)

Describe the roles and responsibilities of the people created by God. (They were to be fruitful and increase in number. They were also responsible for ruling over the rest of God's creation.)

Why do you think God took six days to create the universe? Couldn't He have just put everything in place in a split second? Get several opinions.

Summarize: **Everything God created is good. As He finished His work on the sixth day, God signifies the finality and importance of His creation by saying that it was *very good*. Notice how both creation and reproduction are orderly.**

STEP 4

Personally Designed by God

(Needed: Bibles, copies of Repro Resource 2, paper, pencils)

Refer group members back to Repro Resource 2. Ask: **Do you ever feel empty, void, or disorderly?**
Would you rate your life as being "good"? "Very good"?
If God could spend a day working on you, what might He do? Where might He start?
Your mom and dad had very significant roles in your creation, but what does the fact that God was personally involved in designing the world indicate about His involvement in *your* design?

Have someone read aloud Job 33:4. Emphasize that God was personally active in creation, and His creative power continues today. From the uniqueness of each plant and tree to the individuality shown in the

animal world, God expresses His creativity and His concern for individuals.

Ask: **What is God capable of doing with the chaos and confusion you've identified in your life? Do you think He's at work in you? Why or why not?**

What would you like for God to put in order in your life?

Distribute paper and pencils. Explain: **Many people refuse to see evidence of God in creation. Take a few minutes to think about all of the evidence that you see and appreciate. Then write a short prayer, thanking God for all that He's created. At the end of the prayer, write a few words that express how you feel about God's personal involvement in your own existence.**

IN THE BEGINNING... WHAT? REPRO RESOURCE 1

UDDER CHAOS

IN THE BEGINNING... WHAT?

WHEEL OF LIFE

Divide the wheel according to the amount of time you spend in each of the areas or activities listed below. For example, you might want to allow 8-10 hours for sleeping, 1-2 hours for meals, etc. Then use colored markers to indicate areas of your life that seem snarled, confused, cluttered, or chaotic. You might want to use "warm" colors (reds, oranges, yellows) to indicate severe chaos and "cool" colors (blues, greens, purples) to indicate areas that seem more normal, orderly, or peaceful.

Sleep	Meals	School
Friends	Athletics	Music
TV/radio	Reading	Church-related activities
Bible study	Family time	Work
Other:		

OPTIONS

SESSION ONE

EXTRA ACTION

SMALL GROUP

LARGE GROUP

Extra Action

Step 2
Skip the puzzle. Instead of having kids color the wheel on Repro Resource 2, have them stand at least arm's-length apart. Each person should decide whether to be a Jumper, a Spinner, or a Shaker. Read aloud the categories on Repro Resource 2 (sleep, school, etc.), pausing after each one. Kids are to show physically the chaos level they experience in each area. The more chaotic the area, the higher they jump or the faster they spin or the harder they shake.

Step 4
Bring in poster board, tape, markers, and decorations with an astronomy theme (stick-on stars, stickers depicting the planets, etc.). Have kids make personalized "telescopes" for viewing "the heavenly bodies." When the telescopes are done, ask kids to train them not on the sky, but on each other—as a reminder that our bodies are "heavenly" in the sense that God has made each of us. Point out that we need to remember this when we look at ourselves and when we look at others.

Small Group

Step 1
If you don't have enough group members to make a sock scramble interesting, bring full sets of clothes (T-shirts, shirts, sweatshirts, sweatpants, socks, shoes, overshoes, hats, earmuffs, etc.) instead. If your group is extremely small, scatter one set of clothes randomly around the room, blindfold one volunteer, and time him or her on how long it takes to dress himself or herself properly with verbal instructions from the other group members. Give everyone an opportunity to try; see who has the best time. If your group is large enough, scatter *two* full sets of clothing around the room and let two blindfolded volunteers compete as fellow team members shout instructions to them.

Step 3
If you have fewer than six people, *you* should do the poster drawings for the days of creation not assigned. Another option is to list on the board "Things God Created," but not in the correct order. Individuals can be assigned two or more days to illustrate. After their drawings are finished, various volunteers can then attempt to put them in the correct order.

Large Group

Step 1
Before the session, cut apart large sheets of poster board into several smaller pieces. (Each small piece should be about 8" × 11".) Number each piece. (If you have twenty pieces, number them from one to twenty.) To begin the session, have kids form pairs. Give each pair a piece of poster board and several colored markers. Instruct the pairs to create whatever they want on their pieces of poster board—an abstract drawing, a cartoon, graffiti, or whatever. After a few minutes, collect the pieces. Spread the pictures on the floor in numerical order, as though you're trying to put back together the original sheet of poster board. See how well the pairs' pictures fit together. It's likely that the result will be pretty chaotic. Point out that your group members created chaos from something that was once orderly; God, on the other hand, created order from what was once chaos.

Step 3
Have kids form two teams. Give each team a typewriter, a stack of typing paper, and a large paper grocery bag. Explain that the first person on each team will put the bag over his or her head and type (using only one finger) as fast as he or she can for fifteen seconds. The second person will then put the bag over his or her head and do the same thing. Continue this process until all team members have had a chance to type. Then collect the team's papers. Check them to see how many actual words (of three or more letters) the teams typed. Award prizes to the team with the most words. Afterward, point out that it's pretty hard to put letters in the right order when you leave it to chance. Similarly, it's pretty hard to believe that the orderliness of the universe is the result of chance.

OPTIONS

SESSION ONE

HEARD IT ALL BEFORE

Step 3
Kids may think that going over what happened on the days of creation is for preschoolers. Instead, spend more time on the orderliness of the universe. Bring as many of the following fruits and vegetables as possible: apple, carrot, kiwi fruit, green pepper, okra, celery, garlic, orange, lemon or lime, and tomato. Cut each item in half horizontally. Pass the items around. Encourage kids to look for repeated shapes inside each fruit or vegetable. Ask: **Do the insides of these things look like a chaotic mess, or do you see patterns? How do you think those patterns got there? What does that tell you about the existence of a Creator, and whether He designed things to be orderly?**

Step 4
Even if kids agree that God created the universe, they may doubt that He could be interested in them individually. Challenge kids to do two things at once (walk and chew gum, rub their tummies and pat their heads, comb their hair and recite the names of their schoolteachers, etc.) Point out that most humans can operate on two "tracks" at the same time; surely God is capable of much more. Seeing the "big picture" of the whole universe and the "details" of our lives is no problem for Him.

LITTLE BIBLE BACKGROUND

Step 1
Without being obvious about what you're doing, try to create as much intentional chaos as you can. Rearrange the room. Hide all of the chairs. Meet in an open, noisy place. Have loud music playing as you begin the session. Prearrange with volunteers to begin annoying chatter among themselves whenever you try to say something. Do whatever you think will work for your group, but ignore whatever is going on until kids begin to react to the chaos. Afterward, help your group members see that we may crave more "order" in our lives than we usually admit. Sometimes we tend to resent the fact that God has given us rules to follow for Christian behavior; yet His guidelines are for our own benefit. God isn't on some kind of cosmic power trip. Rather, He knows that we need help eliminating much of the personal chaos in our lives so that we can concentrate on what is really important.

Step 3
To begin this step, ask: **What do your friends say about how life began? What do your science teachers tell you? What do *you* think?** See where your group members stand on this issue. Don't be alarmed if some of them are convinced of the "truth" and "logic" of evolution. Perhaps they have never heard an intelligent presentation of the Creation account. As you lead this session, help kids see the personal and intimate concern that God took when He created the world. It was something He took pride in. The truth of Genesis should be far preferable to the random and impersonal theory of evolution.

FELLOWSHIP & WORSHIP

Step 3
Have your group members stand in a large circle. (You may need to form two or three circles, depending on the size of your group.) Instruct each person to grab one hand of the person standing opposite him or her in the circle and then grab the hand of someone else in the circle. When all hands are joined, instruct group members to untangle themselves—without letting go of each other's hands. It's likely that your group members have done this activity before (after all, it is a youth group "classic"). Help them see that as they untangle the knot, they are in a sense creating order out of chaos—just as God did when He created the world.

Step 4
Explain: **The ultimate creation of all was the creation of humankind. We might sat that this was God's "blue ribbon" work.** Hand out paper and pencils. Instruct group members to write Job 33:4 ("The Spirit of God has made me; the breath of the Almighty gives me life") at the top of their sheet. Then ask: **How does it make you feel to know that the breath of God is what gives you life?** Perhaps some of your group members haven't considered this before. They may have heard that God breathed Adam to life, but may not have thought about themselves. Allow some time for discussion of this principle; then encourage your kids to write, draw, doodle—whatever works best for them—their response to God for giving them the breath of life. Close the session with a time of worship, praising God simply for our lives.

OPTIONS

SESSION ONE

Mostly Girls

Step 2
Girls are much more likely than guys to openly share their areas of concern and chaos. (And junior high girls are likely to have their fair share of chaos in their lives!) After group members have had a few minutes to share a little bit about their color wheels, say: **Let's take a closer look at our areas of chaos and confusion.** As the girls are willing, have them share particular areas that are causing them concern. As they name each area of chaos, write it on the board. When you've collected a fair-sized list, see if you can identify categories into which the chaos areas might fall—schedule chaos, relationship chaos, family chaos, school/grades chaos, and so on. After categorizing the chaos areas, address each category by asking group members to share ways in which they've dealt with similar problems. Afterward, say: **Though a five-minute discussion probably won't turn around our lives or get rid of all of our chaos, just being able to identify the problem is a start.** Make sure your girls know that you're available and willing to talk and pray with them further about their concerns.

Step 4
Take your girls on a short walk outside. Challenge them to find as many different natural textures, colors, shapes, and sizes as they can, and to collect samples of those things that are collectable. (The two-hundred-year-old tree in front of the church is off limits.) After a few minutes, return to your meeting room. Instruct your group members to glue, staple, or tape their natural artifacts to a piece of poster board, creating a "praise mural" for God's creation.

Mostly Guys

Step 2
Most guys don't mind a fairly high level of chaos in their lives. So rather than starting out by trying to help them reduce it, perhaps you will do better by helping them take it to the extreme. Have a King of Chaos contest. Rather than handing out Repro Resource 2, have each person prepare a one-minute speech on why he feels that he should wear the coveted title of "King of Chaos." Each person should explain why his life is more hectic than everyone else's. You should eventually get the same results as you would by using Repro Resource 2. Afterward, explain that while living with chaos can be a benefit or sometimes even a thrill, there are times when chaos gets out of control and a certain degree of order needs to be restored.

Step 4
At the end of the session, try to design a project that will allow your guys to first create chaos out of order, and then order out of chaos. For example, if you need anything demolished and cleared away, your group of guys might be more than willing to comply. See if your church might have an old piano or piece of furniture that it needs to get rid of. If so, provide the proper tools, instructions, and warnings to your group members, and have them create a little chaos. Then be sure to restore order by cleaning up and hauling off all of the pieces. Other projects might include demolition of old sidewalks, removal of trees or fences on church property, the destruction of props left over from the 1962 Christmas play, or any number of things that a group of hyperactive guys might enjoy.

Extra Fun

Step 1
Follow up the sock activity with another fun event. This time, ask everyone to *create* a sock. Provide all sorts of craft materials (clay, construction paper, string, or whatever is available) for kids to work with. If you wish, provide prizes for the most creative sock, the most functional, and so forth. Afterward, point out that while we can't even create a decent sock from existing materials, God created the entire world out of *nothing*.

Step 2
After group members fill out Repro Resource 2, have them pair up to play "Psychiatrist and Patient." One person should play each role. The patient should lie on the floor (in lieu of a couch) and begin by saying, "Doctor, my life is completely too chaotic." Then patients should fill in specific causes of chaos. Each psychiatrist should listen carefully and then offer "professional" advice. After a while, let pairs reverse roles. Call everyone back together and see if anyone received helpful advice. If so, let such people share the advice with the entire group. Group members may surprise themselves with the quality of their advice once the problem of chaotic lives becomes clear to them.

OPTIONS

SESSION ONE

MEDIA

Step 1
Rent the video version of Walt Disney's *Fantasia*. Before the session, fast-forward to the segment depicting the beginnings of the universe (right after the "Sorcerer's Apprentice" with Mickey Mouse, about two-thirds through the tape). The segment begins in outer space, then moves to a chaotic earth full of volcanic activity. Hot lava flows to the sea, where life develops from amoebas to dinosaurs. Play as much of this segment as you have time for. Then ask: **Does this version of life's beginnings look more like the Bible's account or the one you've learned in school? Explain.**

Step 3
Bring a loaded video camera and a tripod. Place chairs in a circle; have kids sit in them. Put the camera on the tripod in a spot that allows you to view the whole circle. Shoot about one second of tape, then stop the camera. Have each person move to the chair on his or her right. Then shoot another second and stop. Repeat the process at least twenty times, moving kids one chair to the right each time you stop the camera. (If your camera has an animation feature, you'll be able to shoot in bursts shorter than one second, which will produce a smoother, faster effect.) Show the results on a monitor. You should see kids "floating" from chair to chair around the circle as if by magic. Ask: **What happened?** Explain that you recorded just part of what took place; you left out the times when kids moved from chair to chair. Note that some people see the biblical days of creation as "snapshots" that hit the highlights and leave out long stretches of time between them; others see them as literal days.

SHORT MEETING TIME

Step 1
Skip Step 1 and the puzzle in Step 2. Start the meeting by showing kids 3-D stereograms from a book like *Hidden Dimensions* by Dan Dyckman (Harmony Books) or from *Games* magazine, which sometimes features one or more stereograms in an issue. Find out whether kids can "bring order out of chaos" by staring at the pictures and seeing the 3-D objects. Then define *chaos* and move into the "Wheel of Life" activity.

Step 3
Instead of using teams, slowly read Genesis 1:3-31 aloud yourself. Give each person a pen and six index cards. As you read, each person should work as quickly as possible to draw each day's creations, one day per card—and then mix up his or her six cards. Have kids pass their cards one person to the right, then try to place in creation-day order the cards they receive. Next, instead of reading the passage again and asking questions about each section, have kids turn to Genesis 1 and answer these questions: **How did God begin creating? What did He do to bring order out of chaos? How did He fill up His empty universe and our world? What did He think of His creations?** Then use the session's questions for Genesis 1:24-31.

URBAN

Step 3
Have your group members act out the six days of creation. Read each of the six sections of Genesis 1 one at a time. When you begin each section, kids should be lying on the floor. As you read each section, they should act out the description of creation. For instance, when you read Genesis 1:4, kids might separate from each other to indicate the separation of light and darkness. When you read Genesis 1:11, kids might pretend to sprout from the ground like vegetation. When you read Genesis 1:16, kids might orbit each other like the moon. Encourage your group members to be creative in their performances.

Step 4
Bring in several newspapers and (if possible) photographs of the neighborhoods in which your group members live. Distribute the papers and photos among your group members. As a group, discuss the various forms of chaos—crime, homelessness, drugs, urban decay, broken families—that surround your kids every day. Ask: **How did this chaos develop in the orderly world that God created?** (The chaos is the result of human sin.) Point out that similar kinds of chaos occur in people's lives because of sin—but that God can bring order to any situation.

OPTIONS

SESSION ONE

Step 2
It's likely that your high schoolers are at a point in their lives when their stressors are increasing quite rapidly. Extracurricular activities require more time; grades really start to count if they're thinking about college; relationships get deeper and more intense; work becomes a factor—not to mention the pressures of drinking, drugs, and premarital sex. Ask a couple of your high schoolers, after sharing their color wheels, to explain exactly how various stressors affect them on a daily basis. The purpose of this sharing time is to give your junior highers, some of whose lives may be almost stress-free, an opportunity to empathize with your high schoolers. Encourage your junior highers to ask questions of the high schoolers regarding major stressors in the high schoolers' lives.

Step 3
Have kids form teams, making sure that you get a balance of junior highers and high schoolers on each team. Ask: **How difficult do you think it is to design or create something?** (Some kids may think there's nothing to it; others may see it as being more difficult.) Say: **We can't create something out of nothing as God did, but we can try to create something out of something.** Give each team a bag filled with all sorts of odds and ends—a potato, a feather duster, paper clips—anything interesting you can find. (Each bag does not need to contain the same items.) Instruct each team to create something from the items in its bag. Offer prizes for the team with the most functional or creative design. Afterward, discuss how difficult it was to build something useful from existing materials; then challenge your kids to think about creating something—life—from nothing.

Step 1
Try a simpler opening activity. Have kids form teams. Give each team a deck of cards. When you give the signal, teams will throw their cards into the air and let them scatter all over the floor. (Be sure to separate the teams so that their cards don't get mixed up.) The teams will then race to pick up their cards and arrange them in a certain order—perhaps hearts first, then spades, then diamonds, and then clubs—with the cards in each suit arranged according to descending value (ace, king, queen, jack, etc.). The first team to hand you its deck of cards arranged correctly is the winner. Use this activity to introduce the idea of creating order out of chaos.

Step 3
Randomly throw out fortune cookies (the kind found in Chinese restaurants) to your group members, making sure that each person gets one cookie. Have kids form pairs. Instruct the members of each pair to break open their cookies and read their fortunes to each other, sharing whether those fortunes apply to them or not. Then have each person give a specific compliment or piece of advice to his or her partner. Afterward, ask kids to compare the two experiences. Suggest that getting a personalized compliment or piece of advice is more meaningful than getting a random fortune from a cookie. Similarly, believing that you were created by a personal God gives your life much more meaning than believing that you're the result of chance.

Date Used:

Approx. Time

Step 1: Ankle-Deep in Chaos _____
o Small Group
o Large Group
o Little Bible Background
o Extra Fun
o Media
o Short Meeting Time
o Sixth Grade
Things needed:

Step 2: Udder Chaos _____
o Extra Action
o Mostly Girls
o Mostly Guys
o Extra Fun
o Combined Junior High/High School
Things needed:

Step 3: Out of Nowhere _____
o Small Group
o Large Group
o Heard It All Before
o Little Bible Background
o Fellowship & Worship
o Media
o Short Meeting Time
o Urban
o Combined Junior High/High School
o Sixth Grade
Things needed:

Step 4: Personally Designed by God _____
o Extra Action
o Heard It All Before
o Fellowship & Worship
o Mostly Girls
o Mostly Guys
o Urban
Things needed:

SESSION 2
The Creation of Man and Woman

YOUR GOALS FOR THIS SESSION:
Choose one or more

☐ To help kids see that human beings are the special creation of God.

☐ To help kids understand the high value God places on each individual.

☐ To help kids begin to value their own specialness because they bear the image of God.

☐ Other _____

Your Bible Base:

Genesis 1:27-31; 2:4-25; 9:6
James 3:9

CUSTOM CURRICULUM

Family Resemblances

(Needed: Paper, pencils, photos of kids' parents, prize)

Before the session, ask group members to bring a picture of their parents to the meeting. Collect and number the photos. Then display them around your meeting area. Give each group member a piece of paper and a pencil. Have kids try to identify which person in the group belongs with the parents in each photo. After everyone has had a chance to record his or her answers, ask kids to reveal which photos are theirs. Award a prize to the person with the most correct matches.

Afterward, ask: **In what ways are you similar to or different from your parents? What's one thing that you are really glad to share in common with your parents?**

Explain: **While your parents created you, you don't necessarily look or act exactly like either or both of them. Sometimes similarities with our parents are outwardly obvious; other times they're not so obvious. Similarly, human beings are like God—our Creator—in some ways, and not like Him in other ways. In this session, we will be examining God's design and purpose for humans as well as what it means to be created in God's image.**

Personal Ads

(Needed: Construction paper, scissors, tape, glue, newspapers, magazines, pencils)

Distribute the collage materials like construction paper, scissors, tape, glue, newspapers, magazines, pencils, etc. Instruct kids to create a brochure advertising themselves. After several minutes, have volunteers display and explain their brochures.

Then ask: **If you were creating an actual brochure for yourself, what one feature or characteristic would you want to make sure you mentioned? Share one thing that you really like about yourself.**

Discuss how the traits shared by group members are expressed in God's own character. Point out that we are special because of our likeness to Him.

Ask kids to share one or two successes in their lives, from age six to the present. Discuss how each success shows the use of some ability given by God, but first found in Him.

Like Father, Like . . . You?

(Needed: Bibles, copies of Repro Resource 3, pencils, prize)

Ask: **What does it mean to be created in God's image?** Explain that like God, we are persons with emotions, values, and choices. Like God, we have identity and individuality. Humans alone share personal attributes with God. To show how the image of God persisted, even after Adam and Eve sinned, have a group member read aloud Genesis 9:6 and James 3:9.

Have the group read Genesis 1:27-31; 2:4-25. Then distribute copies of "The Tree of True and False" (Repro Resource 3). Give group members a few minutes to complete the quiz. After several minutes, review the answers with your kids. The correct answers are as follows: (1) T; (2) F; (3) F; (4) T; (5) F; (6) F; (7) F; (8) F; (9) F; (10) T. Award a prize to the first person who correctly completes the sheet.

Ask: **How did God feel about His creation of man and woman?** (God considered His work on this day *very good*.)

What responsibilities did God give man and woman? How do men and women continue in those responsibilities today? If no one mentions it, explain that God gave humans dominion, the ability to rule. He shared His authority and gave humans the privilege of responsibility. He put humans in a perfect setting—the garden—and instructed them to work and care for it. God knew our need to use our intellect, so He brought all of the animals to the man, giving him the responsibility to name each one. He knew our need for the freedom to choose, so He placed a forbidden tree in the garden. Each of God's actions regarding humans shows that He considers us special and is

C U S T O M   C U R R I C U L U M

OPTIONS

concerned with meeting our needs.

What is significant about God's breathing into man the breath of life? What do we need "breathed" into us now in order to have *eternal* life? Point out that God transformed the form of man into a living, spiritual being capable of having a relationship with Him. With the entrance of sin into the world and God's desire for our repentance through Jesus Christ, He provided a new plan in which the "inbreathing" of the Holy Spirit is necessary for people to again enjoy fellowship with Him.

Why did God create woman? Why do you think God took a rib from Adam to create Eve? Point out that Adam was alone, and that he had a deep need to fill the emptiness in his life. Rather than turning to clay for a second creation, God shaped Eve from Adam so that Adam wouldn't imagine that she was somehow inferior to him. When God sought fellowship, He created man in His own image. But when Adam had a similar need for intimacy, God gave him an even greater gift. The significance of using Adam's rib is that male and female originally shared a oneness. In our present separated existence, we each look to the opposite sex for a form of completion.

What was the man's response to God's gift of a woman? What would your response be if you woke from a nap and discovered that God had made such a gift for you? Point out that Adam recognized and valued Eve as sharing fully in his human identity.

Notice how the man and his wife were naked but felt no shame. What do you think their lack of shame over their nakedness might signify? Is it hard to imagine *not* feeling shame at being naked? Why or why not? Note that Adam and Eve's nakedness suggests that they were at ease with one another without any fears of exploitation or evil. Their lack of shame also probably suggests their lack of sin.

STEP 4

Just a Shadow of Myself

(Needed: Large sheets of paper, colored markers, tape)

Ask: **Is it all right for us to like the good things in ourselves? Why or why not?** Explain that many of us have poor self-images. Sometimes our low self-images are a reflection of excessive criticism

35

from insensitive parents; other times our poor self-views can be attributed to personal failures, bad choices, or sad circumstances. We fail a class in school. We're a little overweight, and others are determined to make us feel self-conscious. Our parents got so involved in the pain of their divorce that they began using us to hurt each other. The list goes on. Ask group members to suggest other possible reasons for a poor self-image.

Then say: **A low self-image is not what God intended. He values each one of us in a special way. To truly understand the creation of man and woman, we must begin to appreciate and understand our own specialness. We should never consider ourselves worthless; we are special because of our likeness to God. It's all right for us to recognize the good in ourselves because we know its source is God. Let's take a few minutes to silently thank God for the gift of His image and for something we really like about ourselves.**

As you wrap up the session, set aside a time for silent prayer. Thank God for helping each group member sense more deeply the reality of His great love.

Then divide the group into pairs. Instruct kids to take turns drawing full-sized silhouettes of their partners on large sheets of paper. These drawings should be taped up around the room and identified. When all of the drawings are displayed, have kids write one feature or characteristic they consider special about each person on his or her silhouette.

Allow kids to take home their silhouettes. Suggest that when they occasionally feel down or "not so special" and they need a self-esteem booster, they should take a look at the special features that other people in the group associate with them. This little reminder may help them recall that God sometimes uses others to remind us that He loves us very much.

IN THE BEGINNING... WHAT?

REPRO RESOURCE 3

THE TREE OF TRUE AND FALSE

Put a T or F in front of each statement to indicate whether you think the statement is true or false.

1. ___ The true identity of human beings is found in creation.

2. ___ Woman is no more than a reflection of man's image.

3. ___ Humans were created to have authority over the beasts of the field, but not the birds in the air.

4. ___ God planned Eden to meet the various needs of Adam's personality.

5. ___ When God created humans, He considered that day of creation so-so.

6. ___ God created woman as a slave to man.

7. ___ God created man and woman on Day 7.

8. ___ Being made in God's image means that we physically look like God.

9. ___ God may have designed human sexuality, but He doesn't necessarily consider it good.

10. ___ God has emotions, values, and creativity.

OPTIONS

SESSION TWO

Extra Action

Step 1
Challenge kids to perform biblical miracles—or at least pale imitations. Have kids form two "miracle-working" teams who will display their skills for the rest of the group. Team A will fill a shallow baking pan with water and try to "part the waters" by blowing on the water in the center of the pan long enough for a Barbie or some other doll to "walk" across. Team B has thirty seconds to break hamburger buns into small pieces and serve a dozen pieces to each group member (adjust the time limit and number of pieces to fit your group's size). If you like, give a prize to the more "miraculous" team. Then ask: **Do we have the same abilities that God does? If not, what does the Bible mean when it says we're created "in His image"? How do we resemble Him?**

Step 3
Seat guys and girls on opposite sides of the room. Explain that the guys are allowed to read only odd-numbered Bible verses and Repro Resource questions. Girls may read only even-numbered ones. Whenever one group comes to a verse or question it can't read, all members of that group must get up, go to the other group, and ask the other group to read the verse or question. After doing this for a while, discuss how much easier it would be if the guys and girls worked together on the same tasks—which is what God intended when He created Adam and Eve.

Small Group

Step 1
The parental photo-identification exercise might not be much of a challenge for a small group, especially since most of the kids are likely to know each other's parents. Instead, hand out pencils and paper. Have group members isolate themselves. Ask everyone to *draw* his or her parent(s). After a few minutes, collect the drawings and post them on the wall. Then let group members guess which picture is whose. Afterward, ask: **What are the best things about your parents? What would you say are some of their worst points? In what ways are you like your parents—either for better or for worse?**

Step 3
Conduct the Bible study and discuss the questions in the session by re-creating the Eden setting. Group members can play the roles of Adam, Eve, God, and perhaps a key animal or two. They should answer the questions in the role of their characters. Perhaps this exercise will help them better appreciate God's original relationship with mankind. If they can begin to see God's intended relationship, they may be more willing to try to re-create that level of intimacy with Him in their personal relationships.

Large Group

Step 3
Give your kids an opportunity to express their creativity in a tasty way. Depending on the time of the day you meet, you'll need to bring in (a) several flavors of ice cream and as many different toppings as you can find, or (b) toaster waffles and as many different toppings as you can find. Encourage your kids to be as creative as possible in preparing their snacks. You might even want to award a prize for the most original (but still edible) creation. Afterward, help kids recognize that our creativity is the result of our likeness to God, the ultimate Creator.

Step 4
The silhouette activity probably won't work well with a large group. Try another self-affirming exercise instead. Give each group member a stamp with a smiling face on it, an inkpad, and a sheet of paper. If you can't find a stamp, give each person a set of several smiling face stickers. Explain that you will be reading a list of personal accomplishments. If an accomplishment applies to a group member, he or she should either stamp or stick a smiling face on his or her paper. In preparing your list of accomplishments, make sure that you cover all kinds of areas so that all of your group members will be able to put several smiling faces on their sheets. (For instance, you might use statements like these: "I've gotten an 'A' on a report card"; "I've hit a home run in a baseball game"; "I've made people laugh"; "I've been told that I have a good personality.") Encourage your kids to keep their sheets so that they can pull them out when they need a self-esteem boost.

OPTIONS

SESSION TWO

HEARD IT ALL BEFORE

Step 3
Whether through repetition or the influence of evolutionary theory, kids may have come to see the story of Adam and Eve as a fairy tale. You don't have time to refute this idea thoroughly, but you can make these points: (1) Several New Testament writers refer to Adam as if he were a real person; Luke even traces the family tree of Joseph back to Adam. (2) Some people who think God may have used evolution to make animals have suggested that Adam and Eve were created separately. (3) Even some who think humans evolved have suggested that Adam and Eve were the first "true" humans, and that the story of God forming them from clay and breathing into them is a symbolic way to describe the fact that they were the only creatures to whom God gave souls. In any case, it's important to remember that Adam and Eve were real, historical people.

Step 4
Kids with self-image problems may be unaffected by the assertion that their "likeness" to God makes them special. Acknowledge that other people, whose opinions of us mean a lot, may not be impressed by the fact that we're made in God's image. It's up to us to remember why we're special. We can also help others stop judging by appearance if we stop judging them. Encourage kids who want others to recognize their inner qualities to start looking for those qualities in others and commenting on them. If you use the silhouette activity, help kids see it as a time to build others up rather than a time to find out how many comments each person can collect.

LITTLE BIBLE BACKGROUND

Step 3
Contrast the biblical account of the creation of Adam and Eve with the current theories of evolution. You may have done this in Session 1 as well. If so, use this time to follow up on questions and comments that weren't adequately covered then. Also, this time focus more on the creation of *people*. Point out that not only was the creation of the *world* personal, but the creation of Adam and Eve was even more so. This is where the theories of evolution break down. The scientific facts of evolution within a species have never translated to the evolution of one-celled animals into human beings. Ask: **Do you think the care that went into the creation of Adam and Eve still goes into every human being, or are we more or less on "automatic pilot" by now?** See Psalm 139:13-16 for insight.

Step 4
If your group members haven't had much Bible background, don't rush through this section. Help kids focus on the self-image issues that are introduced. Your kids may have come into contact with "biblical theology" based on an overemphasis of self-denial. Ask: **When God looks at you, what do you think He sees? Who do you think God loves more—you or Billy Graham? Do you ever blame God when you aren't able to do things that you would like to do—like slam-dunk a basketball or get a certain person's attention?** Try to help group members see that while God creates each person as a unique and distinctive individual, He loves each person unconditionally—no more and no less than anyone else. If you can help your kids see themselves as individually created masterpieces of God's design, perhaps they won't be so reluctant to establish a stronger relationship with their Creator.

FELLOWSHIP & WORSHIP

Step 1
How well do the members of your group really know each other? Have them take a little quiz to find out. Hand out a sheet of paper and a pencil to each person. Ask group members to write down three things about themselves that they really like, that are unique, or that others might find interesting. (This may be difficult for junior highers, so give them as much encouragement as possible.) After kids have completed their lists, instruct them to write their names on their sheets; then collect the papers. Read each list aloud; then ask group members to guess whose it is. Write down the various guesses. After you've read all of the descriptions, go back through and identify who wrote each list. Kids may be surprised to discover the results. To continue the "getting to know you" theme, introduce the family-picture activity.

Step 4
Have your group members sit in a circle on the floor. Say: **We've talked a little bit about why some people have poor self-images, and we've spent a little time identifying the good that God has created in us. Now let's think about the things that cause us to get down on ourselves and offer them to God to remove from our lives.** Allow a few minutes of silent prayer for kids to share their hurts with God. Close the session by having kids listen to or sing "I Cast All My Cares upon You."

OPTIONS

S E S S I O N   T W O

Step 2
After your girls have finished their brochures, say: **Now let's put together a brochure featuring what society would describe as the "perfect" female.** Have kids form pairs. Give each pair a few minutes to create a "perfect female" brochure. When everyone is finished, have each pair present its brochure. Then discuss as a group the expectations—both realistic and unrealistic—placed on females in our society. Ask your girls to share their feelings about these expectations. Then ask: **Do you think such a perfect person exists?** (Obviously not.) **What do you think God expects of us?** If no one mentions it, point out that He loves us regardless of how we do or don't measure up to society's yardstick. His expectations of us are to love and follow Him.

Step 4
Give each of your group members a small, inexpensive hand or pocket mirror. Then set out a variety of paints on a table. Say: **God created you exactly the way He wanted you to be—the way He knew was perfect for you.** Allow some time for your group members to paint on their mirrors a reminder—perhaps a word, pictures, or design—of the fact that God loves them just the way they are. Say: **Every time you use this mirror from now on, remember that God made you to be who you are, and that He loves you.**

Step 2
As your guys prepare their personal ads, instruct them to design something that might appear in a singles magazine or the singles section of a newspaper. When they get finished, let volunteers share what they have written. Then ask: **What changes would you make if the information were to be submitted on a job application instead? How about a college-entrance application? Signing up for a short-term Christian mission project?** Help your guys see that they can draw on a variety of strengths, depending on the need at hand. They should also see that what they consider to be physical strengths are not likely to be as important in the big picture of life as other character traits and inner qualities.

Step 3
Discuss the fact that Adam and Eve could walk around naked without feeling shame. Ask: **Is this possible today? Can you think of anyone of the opposite sex with whom you would feel comfortable walking around naked? What causes us to get shameful or giggly when it comes to issues of sex, nudity, and so forth?** Perhaps your guys will be honest about how their thoughts are influenced by dirty jokes, peer pressure, and pornography. Explain that one of Satan's most common strategies is to pervert something good that God provides. Drinking fine wine with meals can develop into drunkenness or alcoholism; eating good food can become gluttony; success in business can lead to greed; and the God-given sexual drive that should lead to a lifetime commitment to a single marriage partner can result in a variety of sexual sins. Many of your guys are likely to believe that looking at pornography is "something all guys do" and that it has little consequence. Try to show how pornography degrades not only women as a gender, but also God's plan for men and women.

Step 2
To expand on the idea of making brochures for the purpose of advertising oneself, ask kids to make Personality Donor Cards. These should be a combination of an organ donor card and a senior will (in which seniors bequeath to underclassmen essentials for high school that the seniors will no longer need). For example, a Personality Donor Card might say something like "When I die, I would like _____ to inherit my sense of humor because she always seems so serious" or "I want to donate my cranky morning attitude to _____ because she is always so happy." After a few minutes, have each person read his or her donor card. This activity is designed to help kids recognize how many positive traits they possess.

Step 4
Give your kids a "trademark quiz." Bring in a number of products or company logos with the name marked out or taped over. Identify the items only by number; see how many your kids can identify. (If you use a Polaroid camera on the way to the meeting, you might also get shots of a number of hotel chains, gas stations, restaurants, and other recognizable trademarks to use.) Most of what you bring should be fairly easy for kids to identify; a few items should be tougher. After the quiz, point out how easy it is to identify certain products simply by colors of packaging, type styles, and other simple means. Then explain that God's people have a common mark—His Spirit (Romans 8:16). The presence of the Holy Spirit is a uniting bond we share. But God also gives us each a unique "trademark"—our fingerprints, which differentiate us from anyone else who has ever lived. As a conclusion to this exercise, pull out an ink pad and let group members add their fingerprints to the silhouette sheets they made.

OPTIONS

SESSION TWO

MEDIA

Step 2
Instead of having kids make brochures promoting themselves, run a "video dating service." Bring a video camera; tape three volunteers sitting in front of the camera, one at a time, answering these questions about themselves: **Why would someone have a great time by going out with you? What is one of your best features? Would you go out with "just anybody," or does the person need to meet certain standards? Why?** Then play back the tape. Let the group award a prize to the person who best displayed "self-esteem above and beyond the call of duty."

Step 4
Play a "secular" song that seems to show high self-esteem on the part of the singer(s). Some past examples include "Greatest Love of All" (Whitney Houston), "I'm Too Sexy" (Right Said Fred), "We Built This City" (Starship), "I Will Survive" (Gloria Gaynor), "Material Girl" (Madonna), "Flashdance . . . What a Feeling" (Irene Cara), and "I Get Around" (The Beach Boys). Contrast that song with a contemporary Christian song that gives a reason for having healthy self-esteem. Some examples include "So Glad I Know" (Deniece Williams), "That's Where the Joy Comes From" (Steve Green), "Maker of My Heart" (Glad), "We Are the Reason" (David Meece), and "All Things Are Possible" (Dan Peek). Ask: **Is it better to think you're special because of your looks or talents, or because of what God thinks of you? Why?**

SHORT MEETING TIME

Step 1
Replace Steps 1 and 2 with a shorter opener. Have kids form pairs. Partners should listen as you tell this story: **Dr. Erwin Nutcase, mad scientist, has been trying to create a clone of each person in this group. But something went wrong, probably because he bought his DNA from the Home Shopping Network. He got one clone for every two group members—with half the personality traits of each person in your pair. Knowing that, decide what your clone would do (a) when threatened by a gang member, and (b) after winning a million-dollar sweepstakes prize.** After letting pairs talk this over for two minutes, share results. Then discuss what it means to be created in someone's image.

Step 3
Skip the quiz on Repro Resource 3. Also skip Genesis 9:6 and James 3:9. Have half of your group look at Genesis 1:27-31 and the other half look at Genesis 2:4-25 (but skip 2:10-14). Rather than using the somewhat complex discussion questions in the session, ask both groups to summarize what happened in the passages and in what ways Adam and Eve may have been created "in God's image." (They were to "create" new life by multiplying; they were rulers; they had work to do; they could make choices; they could love and communicate; they were to be concerned with right and wrong; etc.)

URBAN

Step 1
If many of your kids come from broken homes, the parent-picture activity may not be a good idea. Try another opener instead. Ask volunteers to do some impersonations for the group. Kids may impersonate celebrities, each other, or you. Emphasize that none of the impersonations should be hurtful or embarrassing. After each volunteer finishes his or her performance, discuss how much he or she looked or sounded like the person being imitated. Use this activity to lead in to a discussion of how much we're like God, our Creator.

Step 3
To give your group members an idea of the amazing brainpower it took to name the animals in the Garden of Eden, let kids do some naming of their own. Bring in several pictures of unusual and extraordinary animals—creatures that your kids probably haven't seen or heard of before. As you hold up each picture, have group members call out names for the animal. Emphasize that the names should be completely original, and not simply variations of existing animal names. Vote as a group on the best name for each animal; then compare that name to the animal's actual name.

OPTIONS

S E S S I O N   T W O

Step 1
Divide your group into two teams—a team of junior highers and a team of high schoolers. (It doesn't matter if the teams aren't even.) Give each team a piece of poster board and some markers. Instruct the teams to list as many completions as possible to the following sentence starter: "God made humans . . . " After a few minutes, have each team share its list. Ask: **What similarities are there between these lists? What differences are there?** Allow time for discussion. Then say: **God created humans in His image to love Him and others. How we do that changes or varies with our age, experience, and background. What matters is that He loves us and wants us to love Him—and each other—in return.**

Step 4
Some of your high schoolers may need a refresher course in the difference between being prideful and having a healthy self-esteem. Some of your junior highers may need some help understanding the difference. On two large sheets of paper, draw the outlines of two bodies (one per sheet). Under one outline, write "Arrogant"; under the other, write "Healthy Self-Image." Separate your junior highers and high schoolers. Give each group a set of markers. Hand one of the outlines to each group. Give each group thirty seconds to fill in as many traits as it can think of that fit that category; then switch the outlines and give each group thirty more seconds to work. After both groups have had a chance to write on each outline, discuss group members' ideas of what it means to have a healthy self-image and what it means to be arrogant.

Step 2
Your sixth graders may not know enough about advertising techniques and principles to create brochures for themselves. Instead, ask them to think of the three words or phrases that best describe them. Then, as a group, discuss how each person's traits are expressed in God's own character. Help your group members see that their positive characteristics are the result of their likeness to God.

Step 3
The quiz on Repro Resource 3 may be too difficult for some of your sixth graders. Try using the following questions instead. Have kids stand up if they think the answer is true, sit on the floor if they think it's false, and squat halfway down if they're unsure. The questions are as follows:
- **Because the woman was created after the man, she meant less to God than the man did.** (False.)
- **God has emotions.** (True.)
- **God was less pleased with what He created on the sixth day than He was with His earlier work.** (False.)
- **Being made in God's image means that we physically look like God.** (False.)
- **Being made in God's image means that we're special.** (True.)

Date Used: Approx. Time

Step 1: Family Resemblances   _____
o Extra Action
o Small Group
o Fellowship & Worship
o Short Meeting Time
o Urban
o Combined Junior High/High School
Things needed:

Step 2: Personal Ads   _____
o Mostly Girls
o Mostly Guys
o Extra Fun
o Media
o Sixth Grade
Things needed:

Step 3: Like Father, Like . . . You?   _____
o Extra Action
o Small Group
o Large Group
o Heard It All Before
o Little Bible Background
o Mostly Guys
o Short Meeting Time
o Urban
o Sixth Grade
Things needed:

Step 4: Just a Shadow of Myself   _____
o Large Group
o Heard It All Before
o Little Bible Background
o Fellowship & Worship
o Mostly Girls
o Extra Fun
o Media
o Combined Junior High/High School
Things needed:

SESSION 3: The Creation of Rest and Worship

YOUR GOALS FOR THIS SESSION:

Choose one or more

☐ To help kids see what God did at the completion of His creation.

☐ To help kids understand the importance of rest and worship.

☐ To help kids begin to set aside time to rest and worship.

☐ Other _____

Your Bible Base:

Genesis 2:1-3
Exodus 20:8-10
Psalm 95:1-7

OPTIONS

STEP 1

Give It a Rest!

(Needed: Instrumental music, tape player, copies of Repro Resource 4, pencils)

As group members arrive, have some kind of instrumental music playing. Ask kids to quietly lie down on the floor, close their eyes, and rest. After kids have had a few minutes to rest, turn down the music and ask them to remain lying down with their eyes closed. Then say: **Raise your hand if this is the first time you've had to rest all day.** Allow time for responses.

Then say: **Call out some words or phrases that describe how the last few minutes have felt to you.** (Descriptive words might include peaceful, sleepy, quiet, boring, etc.)

Hand out copies of "The Rest of the Sentence" (Repro Resource 4) and pencils. Give kids a few minutes to complete the statements about rest. Afterward, go through the sheet as a group, asking several volunteers to share their responses to each statement. Be prepared to share your own responses to the statements as well.

Then ask: **When was the last time you felt truly rested? If it's been a while, why do you think it's been so long? If you feel that you get plenty of rest, why do you think rest comes so easily to you?** Encourage most of your group members to respond.

STEP 2

God's Day Off

(Needed: Bibles)

Say: **Let's read Genesis 2:1-3 to see how God feels about rest.** Have someone read aloud the passage.

Then ask: **Why do you think God rested on the seventh day? Was it because He was worn out?** Point out that God had finished with the work of creation. Nothing remained formless or empty as was

45

discussed in Session 1 of this book.

Say: **Notice that, in verse 3, the Creator rested and commemorated—or celebrated—the perfection of His creation.**

Have someone read aloud Exodus 20:8-10. Then ask: **What's going on in this passage?** If no one mentions it, point out that God's moral Law is found in the Ten Commandments, which were given to Moses as he led God's people out of Egypt. Commandment #4 is one of the first times the word *sabbath* is used in the Old Testament. Explain that the Hebrew verb translated "rested" is the origin of the noun *sabbath*. Keeping the sabbath involved remembering and honoring God.

Say: **Scripture informs us that we are to rest from our own work or activity, just as God did from His.**

Ask group members to think about what part(s) of their lives God might like them to slow down. What do they need to do in order to rest? Go to bed earlier? Cut out one afterschool event a week or month? Encourage your kids to listen for God's direction as you continue this session.

Who or What Do You Worship?

(Needed: Copies of Repro Resource 5, pencils)

Explain: **For us to enter God's rest means we must learn to be responsive to Him and let His Word guide us.**

Distribute copies of "My Guiding Light" (Repro Resource 5) and pencils. Say: **Let's look at the "guiding light" of your life. Draw a picture in the lighthouse of the things or people that are most important to you. Be honest.** After group members finish their drawings, ask volunteers to display and explain their "guiding lights."

Then ask: **Why is it sometimes hard to let God have first place in our lives?** Get several responses.

Then suggest: **It must be frustrating to God when we allow things to get in the way of His having first place in our lives. Responding to God means worshiping Him. If we don't take time to rest, we probably won't take time to worship Him. Worship means valuing God for who He is and focusing our attention on Him.**

How can we focus our attention on Him if we never pause to consider Him or His desires for us? When was the last

time you thought about how God wanted you to spend your day of worship?

STEP 4

For Better or Worship

(Needed: Bibles, paper, pencils, hymnals or songbooks, colored markers)

Have kids form small groups. Assign each group one or more of the following worship elements. Explain: **Church worship services in New Testament times usually included lessons from what we know as the Old Testament, prayers, hymns, remembrance of Christ's death, communion, and the sharing of material possessions. We're going to close this session with a short worship service using some of those elements. As we plan and participate in this time of worship, ask yourself: What about God or His creation really moves me?**

Group 1 will present a creative reading of Psalm 95:1-7.

Group 2 will choose and be prepared to lead some hymns and songs that focus on the passage from Psalm 95.

Group 3 will write several individual prayers and plan a prayer exercise for the entire group.

Group 4 will explore ways to worship through creative arts—drawings, graffiti, poetry, etc.

If time permits, close your session with the worship service your group members have prepared. You might want to use the following order: reading from Psalm 95:1-7; individual prayers; hymns and songs; creative arts expressions; corporate prayer.

If you don't have enough time to worship in this session, plan a special time of worship during which your kids can experience the service they have planned.

Conclude the session by asking group members to silently complete the following statement: **This week I will worship God by . . .**

IN THE BEGINNING... WHAT?   REPRO RESOURCE 4

THE REST OF THE SENTENCE

1. When I want to kick back, I . . . *(circle as many as are appropriate)*

- take a nap in front of the TV
- read a good book
- go to the movies
- spend time with my family
- attend church
- go for a walk
- visit relatives
- hang out with my girlfriend or boyfriend
- play with my pet
- shoot hoops with friends
- attend a sporting event
- do homework
- listen to music
- go on a picnic
- talk on the phone
- go to the beach
- play the piano (or some other musical instrument)
- other:

2. Sundays at my house are . . .

3. My idea of a restful Sunday afternoon is . . .

4. To really feel rested in the morning, I probably need ___ more hour(s) of sleep than the ___ hours I'm currently getting.

5. In order to really feel rested at the end of the week, I probably need to stop . . .

6. A whole day of rest for me would be . . .

IN THE BEGINNING... WHAT? REPRO RESOURCE 5

MY GUiDiNG LiGHT

OPTIONS

SESSION THREE

EXTRA ACTION

Step 1
Have kids form three groups. Instruct Group 1 to play a physically active game (table tennis, dodge ball, etc.); instruct Group 2 to play a mentally challenging game (charades, guessing state capitals, etc.); instruct Group 3 to look at comic books. After two minutes, have groups trade activities. After two minutes, switch again so that all groups will have tried all three activities. Then ask: **Which of these activities would you call "rest"? Why?** Discuss the differences between rest (a break that recharges us) and entertainment (sometimes just a distraction). Point out that most of us know more about entertainment than we do about true rest. In Step 2, have kids run in place whenever verses are read and rest during discussion.

Step 3
Place a "throne" chair in the middle of the room. Tie half a dozen balloons to the seat. Have three "kings" vie to sit on the throne. They may not use hands or feet to push the others away—only rear ends. Whoever's sitting on the throne when the balloons are all popped is the "king." Ask the group: **Do you want to bow down to this king? Why or why not?** Use this activity to introduce the idea of choosing who we worship.

SMALL GROUP

Step 3
When the topic turns to worship in a small group, a question that frequently comes to mind (though may remain unasked) is "Why bother?" Don't let the question remain unspoken. Ask: **If only a handful of people are willing to come to this group, why should the few of us go to all the trouble? Why not just go out in our backyard or to a local park to worship on our own? Wouldn't God get just as much glory? It would certainly be more convenient for us, wouldn't it?** Let kids respond. After your discussion, try to encourage your kids with the following Scripture passages:
• Hebrews 10:24, 25—Corporate worship is not only for God's benefit; it also allows us to "spur one another on toward love and good deeds."
• I Corinthians 12:12-26—We are all parts of a bigger "body." To neglect our own gifts and responsibilities is to cause the entire body to suffer.

Step 4
When you plan the worship service, you aren't likely to be able to form groups to prepare for each step. Rather, in a small group these responsibilities will probably fall upon individuals. So make it clear that individuals need not *do* everything. Their goal should be to create ways to get everyone involved in whatever portion of the worship service they are preparing. For example, the person assigned to read Psalm 95:1-7 might ask each of the other kids to read one or two verses. The hymns and prayers naturally include everybody. Anything that is done should be designed to accommodate the entire group. Too often, creative worship becomes little more than entertainment, with one "performer" and the others serving as a captive audience. Help your kids be alert to the worship needs of the entire group.

LARGE GROUP

Step 1
As your group members are relaxing, ask volunteers to stand and share stories of when they were the most tired they've ever been. For instance, someone might tell of being exhausted after running in a long-distance race. Someone else might tell of being incredibly sleepy after staying up all night. You might consider awarding a prize for the best story. Afterward, ask your volunteers to describe how it felt to rest after being so tired.

Step 3
The worship activity in Step 4 gives group members an opportunity to *corporately* commemorate and worship God, but what about ideas for individual worship and commemoration? Have kids form groups. Instruct each group to brainstorm a list of specific, creative things a person could do on his or her day of rest to commemorate God. See which group can come up the most ideas. (With a large group, you should get a wealth of creative ideas.) After a few minutes, have each group share its list. Instruct your kids to jot down any ideas that sound interesting to them. Encourage them to use at least a few of the ideas on their next day of rest.

OPTIONS

SESSION THREE

HEARD IT ALL BEFORE

Step 2
Kids may have a "so what?" attitude toward the subject of the sabbath. Why worry about *one* day of rest when we have whole *weekends* for that? Have kids brainstorm lists of things that they typically do on weekends. Then ask how many of those things are actually rest (as opposed to entertainment, chores, time-fillers, etc.) and how many of those things focus their attention on God. Explain that there's a big difference between sabbath rest—pausing from the work of the rest of the week and taking time to worship—and the way many of us spend our weekends.

Step 4
Longtime church attenders may see the mini-worship service as simply another boring example of "playing church." Take away as many traditional "worship props" as possible (hymnals, chorus books, Bibles, etc.) and assign teams to come up with a form of worship that isn't usually used in your church. These might involve bowing down to show reverence, leading a cheer, acting out a Bible story from memory, etc.

LITTLE BIBLE BACKGROUND

Step 2
Kids with a limited Bible background (and even those who are regular church attenders) may have a question at this point. To help them verbalize it, ask: **Which is it? Are we supposed to *rest* on Sunday? Or are we supposed to drag ourselves out of bed to get to Sunday school, church, and perhaps Sunday night services? How can we rest with all of this activity going on? And besides, is resting on Sunday still expected? Haven't times changed so that no one really buys into that "day of rest" concept anymore?** Help guide the discussion so that kids begin to see a difference between doing nothing and actively *resting in God*. Explain that most of us need a little help to stay focused on God when we suddenly stop doing what we've been working on so hard during the week. That's one of the purposes of corporate worship, and why we should commit our Sundays to church activities.

Step 3
As your group members illustrate their priorities on Repro Resource 5, they may not come up with the expected Christian responses of "God," "family," "church," and so forth. Be sensitive to where your kids are. Help them know for sure that God is a caring, loving, giving Father who will take good care of them when no one else is willing or able to. Therefore, they should seek His will and learn to place Him at the top of their priority lists. God knows what your kids want and need. When they learn to put Him first, then many of the things they listed will be given to them as well (Matthew 6:33).

FELLOWSHIP & WORSHIP

Step 1
After your group members have had a minute or two to rest, turn their rest time into a worship time. Allow the music to continue playing as you softly read Psalm 46:10 ("Be still, and know that I am God"). Instruct your group members to do as the psalm says. After a few more minutes, ask: **How easy or difficult was it to be still and think about who God is?** (Most of your group members, if they're honest, will admit that it was a challenge.) Move on to Repro Resource 4 and continue Step 1 as written.

Step 4
Rather than (or in addition to) having group members plan and implement a worship service themselves, you might plan to attend as a group a worship service at another church in your community. Point out that God is a God of creativity and variety, and sometimes it's good for us to open our eyes to the ways others worship Him.

OPTIONS

SESSION THREE

Mostly Girls

Step 1
Distribute crayons, markers, colored paper, scissors, tape, glue, paints, clay—anything falling into the category of "creative materials." Say: **God created rest. It's something good that He wanted us to have. Now we're going to create something to remind us to rest.** Instruct group members to draw, paint, sculpt, or write something that represents rest to them. It might be a drawing of a peaceful scene by a lake, a paper sculpture of a tree, a clay model of a dog—anything that represents rest (or restful play) is an option. After your girls have finished their creations, encourage them to take their work home as a reminder that God wants us to rest.

Step 3
Bring in some inexpensive kaleidoscopes (small plastic ones). Give one to each of the girls in your group. Instruct group members to look at you through their kaleidoscopes. As they do, hold up several objects (that you've had out of sight) for them to identify. Your group members probably won't be able to recognize the objects through their kaleidoscopes. Afterward, say: **We often have so many things going on in our lives that it's hard for us to stop and focus on the one that's most important—God. In order to rest and worship, we need to periodically clear the clutter out of our lives and refocus on Him.** Encourage your girls to take home their kaleidoscopes as a reminder to focus more on God.

Mostly Guys

Step 1
Ask your guys: **Isn't resting—doing nothing—a wimpy thing to do? Isn't it the same as being lazy and undisciplined? What do the following people say or do if they catch you doing nothing: coaches? teachers? parents? employers? What do their responses to your inaction suggest about rest?** While laziness and lack of discipline may indeed be problems for a few of your kids, group members should see that some people will never understand the principle of taking time out of a busy schedule simply to rest. Encourage kids to seek out a time and place where they can incorporate rest on a regular basis without being interrupted by outside people or problems.

Step 4
Your guys may find it a bit awkward to put together their own worship service, but don't let them slide. Instead, have them plan a male-oriented service. Hymns might include low-voiced rounds or topical songs along the lines of "Rise Up, O Men of God." The discussion and application of Scripture can be much more focused. Even the "creative arts" portion could be structured around things that your guys are familiar with. For example, spiritual growth is frequently compared to sports (boxing, wrestling, running a race, etc.) or fighting. With a little effort, your guys should be able to create a very unique worship service and not feel nearly as uncomfortable as they might expect.

Extra Fun

Step 1
Begin the session by announcing a "rest contest." Explain that the people who best demonstrate "resting" will be rewarded. The competitive natures of your group members are likely to be frustrated when the goal is doing nothing. This activity will also let you see if any of your kids are wise enough to know that "rest" can also include any number of things: reading, walking around, conversing, playing board games, or whatever. After you get some idea of how your group members define resting, reward them all with the opportunity to rest without the pressures of competition. Play the music you've prepared, let kids stretch out on the floor, and carry on the session as written.

Step 4
Frequently youth group meetings are action-oriented. Leaders tend to think that the more frenzied the meeting, the better. But kids also need good, restful events from time to time. Plan an evening of rest and try to implement it at an especially effective time (during exam week, right after SATs, etc.). Keep the event as low-key as possible. Watch TV. Play some videos. Pull out the board games. Let kids generate as many ideas as they can think of. To make this activity fun *now*, toss out handfuls of wrapped candy for every good idea that is provided.

OPTIONS

SESSION THREE

MEDIA

SHORT MEETING TIME

URBAN

Step 1
Show a video of a high-energy TV sitcom that you've recorded—but show it on fast-forward. After a minute or so, discuss how it felt to watch the quick, jumpy movements. Do kids ever feel their lives are that way? If so, when? When do they most need to rest? How did kids feel when you stopped the tape? If kids could put their lives on "pause" for awhile, would they do it? Why or why not?

Step 4
Bring several recorded praise songs. Have kids look at the lyrics on the liner notes or listen to parts of the songs in order to become familiar with them. Then have kids vote to choose the three songs that most move them to worship God. Play the three songs; then close in prayer. Some songs to consider are "Sing Your Praise to the Lord," "El Shaddai," and "What a Difference You've Made in My Life" (Amy Grant); "Hosanna," "Great Is the Lord," and "To the Praise of His Glorious Grace" (Michael W. Smith); "Star of the Morning" (Leon Patillo); "Hymn" (Randy Stonehill); "Let the Whole World Sing" (DeGarmo and Key); "Celebrate" (Teri DeSario); and "Heavenly Father" (Billy Sprague).

Step 1
Skip Step 1. Go directly to the Step 2 Bible study. Every time you ask a question or give an instruction to read a verse, change your mind and say that the group's been working too hard and deserves a break. Proceed to read the verse or answer the question yourself. When you reach the end of the step, when kids are asked to consider how they need to rest, point out that this is something you can't do for them; they need to listen for God's direction themselves during the remainder of the session.

Step 4
Skip the worship service. Instead, play calming instrumental music while each person writes on an index card what he or she plans to do for the rest of the day. Have kids write a question mark next to any activity that they're not sure God would approve of; have them write an exclamation point next to any activity that's likely to provide more stress than rest. Encourage kids to discuss these cards with their parents later, and to adjust their plans if possible.

Step 3
Bring photos (from magazines, family albums, etc.) of ten activities in which kids might take part on a Sunday (reading the comics, hang gliding, going to church, eating, watching TV, etc.). Display the photos on the wall in pairs. Have kids walk around, look at the photos, and vote on which of the two activities in each pair is (a) more restful, and (b) more likely to bring a person closer to God. Don't be surprised if there's strong disagreement; simply encourage kids to explain their votes. Then ask: **How might your attitude while taking part in these activities make a difference in whether they're restful? How might it make a difference in whether they help you get closer to God?**

Step 4
Adjust the group assignments for the worship activity at the end of the session to fit the worship styles and interests of your group members. For instance, you might ask the members of Group 1 to share, after reading Psalm 95:1-7, which elements of God's creation they're most thankful for and why. You might ask the members of Group 2 to create a rap that deals with creation and teach it to the rest of the group. Encourage all of your group members to customize their assignments to fit their personal worship styles.

OPTIONS

SESSION THREE

Step 2
In our fast-paced, hectic, instant-everything society, it takes a lot of effort to *think* about the concept of resting, much less to actually *do* it. Have kids form two teams—a team of junior highers and a team of high schoolers. Give each team a piece of paper and a pencil. Instruct each team to brainstorm a list of all of the barriers they can think of that prevent them from resting. After a few minutes, have each group share its list. There will probably be some notable differences between the two lists. Say: **Even now, your lives are filled with all kinds of activities and responsibilities that make it hard to rest. The sad thing is that the older we get, the longer our list of barriers grows. But the good news is that God knew that would happen, so He set aside an entire day for us to use for rest. We just need to take Him up on the offer.**

Step 3
Write the following verse on a large piece of paper or poster board for the entire group to see: "This is what worship is all about. It is not confined to loud singing or verbal exclamations. It is turning our hearts, minds, and bodies over to God's ownership, and dedicating our abilities and gifts to His service" (Author unknown). Ask:
After reading this, do you think our worship should be limited to Sundays only? (No, we are to worship God with all of our lives, every day.)
What part of your heart, mind, or body can you turn over to God's ownership today? Ask kids to reflect silently on this question, without answering it out loud.

Step 1
Probably the last thing your sixth graders are interested in doing is lying quietly on the floor with their eyes closed. So begin the session with a vigorous aerobics workout. If you're up to it, lead the workout yourself; if not, use an aerobics video workout. Keep your group members moving—jumping, running in place, etc.—non-stop for five minutes (or until they're completely worn out). While they're resting from their workout, have them complete Repro Resource 4. Then continue the rest of the session as written.

Step 2
To help your sixth graders better understand the idea of commemorating God on our day of worship, have them consider some other things that are commemorated. Ask: **How do we commemorate the men and women who gave their lives for our country?** (On Memorial Day, parades are held in their honor.)
How do we commemorate the founding of our nation? (On the Fourth of July, fireworks displays are held in celebration of America's independence.)
How do we commemorate Jesus' birth? (At Christmas, we sing carols and put up nativity scenes as a reminder of Christ's birth.) Then ask: **How should we commemorate God on our day of rest?**

Date Used:

Approx. Time

Step 1: Give It a Rest! ____
o Extra Action
o Large Group
o Fellowship & Worship
o Mostly Girls
o Mostly Guys
o Extra Fun
o Media
o Short Meeting Time
o Sixth Grade

Step 2: God's Day Off ____
o Heard It All Before
o Little Bible Background
o Combined Jr. High/High School
o Sixth Grade

Step 3: Who or What Do You Worship? ____
o Extra Action
o Small Group
o Large Group
o Little Bible Background
o Mostly Girls
o Urban
o Combined Jr. High/High School

Step 4: For Better or Worship ____
o Small Group
o Heard It All Before
o Fellowship & Worship
o Mostly Guys
o Extra Fun
o Media
o Short Meeting Time
o Urban

SESSION 4
The Creation of a New Plan

YOUR GOALS FOR THIS SESSION:
Choose one or more

☐ To help kids see that Adam and Eve introduced sin and death into the world.

☐ To help kids understand that God's plan involves Christ's bringing righteousness and life into the world.

☐ To help kids affirm that through Christ we can establish a personal relationship with God.

☐ Other _____

Your Bible Base:

Genesis 2:15-17; 3:1-24
John 3:16
Romans 5:12, 18

CUSTOM CURRICULUM

OPTIONS

STEP 1

Choose Your Own Endings

(Needed: Copies of Repro Resource 6)

Ask for several volunteers to roleplay the situations on "What Would You Do?" (Repro Resource 6). Hand out copies of the sheet to your volunteers and assign roles. Give the actors a few minutes to prepare; then have them perform the roleplays. In the midst of wild applause from the rest of the group for the roleplay performances, ask your actors: **What kinds of reactions did you have when you were caught in the act? Did any of you try to lie your way out of the situation? Why or why not? Did any of you try to justify your actions? Why or why not?**

Ask the rest of the group: **Did you see any evidence that the characters were feeling guilty? Did anyone attempt to hide the truth or deceive by only telling part of the truth?**

If no one mentions it, say: **Notice how easily the feelings of guilt and shame arise. Today, we will look at the historical origin of these feelings and the impact of sin on our relationship with God.**

STEP 2

Not Off to a Very Good Start

(Needed: Bibles, copies of Repro Resource 7, pencils)

Have kids form three teams to study the origin of sin. Distribute copies of "Truth and Consequences" (Repro Resource 7) and pencils. Assign each team one section of the sheet to study. After several minutes, reassemble the group. Ask a member from each team to report his or her team's findings. Use the following information to supplement your discussion of the sheet.

Temptation

1. The fact that the snake came unexpectedly and in disguise sug-

gests that this may be the nature of temptation. Ask your group members to talk about times when they've faced unexpected temptations.

2. The one element of truth in the serpent's lie was that Adam's and Eve's eyes would be opened and they would become like God. However, this statement is only half true. While their eyes were opened to a new awareness of themselves, they no longer retained their moral innocence.

3. Eve added the phrase, "and you must not touch it" (Genesis 3:3), to God's directive.

4. The serpent convinced Eve that she and Adam could do a better job of being God than God could. He persuaded them to depend on themselves instead of on God to meet their needs.

5. Eve and Adam hoped to gain wisdom.

6. The consequence of disobeying God was an immediate awareness of their uneasiness around each other and around God.

Confrontation

7. A few words that might describe Adam's and Eve's first impulse on hearing God in the garden are *shame, guilt, embarrassment, fear, conflict,* etc.

8. God approached Adam and Eve with a question, drawing them out of their hiding. Rather than angrily condemning them, He allowed them to admit the truth of what they had done.

9. Adam tried to shift responsibility for his disobedience by blaming Eve and, ultimately, God.

Judgment

10. The serpent is cursed and sentenced to crawl as a reminder of temptation. In addition, God indicates that there will be a struggle between people and snakes throughout history. Pain in childbearing is God's sentence for Eve. In addition, God indicates that there will be a struggle between men and women because of their self-centered cores. Finally, Adam's sentence is the exchange of working in a beautiful, pleasant garden to painfully working hard ground cursed with thorns and thistles. However, God, in His grace, allows Adam to produce food that will sustain his life.

11. In Genesis 3:15, God promises that the offspring of the woman would eventually crush the serpent's head, a promise fulfilled by Christ, who defeated Satan.

12. God expressed His love and care by providing Adam and Eve with more effective clothing than fig leaves. In this way, He showed that He cared about their immediate physical needs as well as their ultimate spiritual needs. Later, animal sacrifice became the commanded form of approaching God and dealing with sin.

13. God was gracious in not allowing Adam and Eve to live forever in their chaotic state. Their banishment from the garden prevented them from eating from the tree of life and living forever.

Summarize: **While Adam and Eve introduced sin and death**

into the world, God already had a plan to bring righteousness and life into the world. To see what that plan was, let's read Romans 5:12, 18. Have a group member read aloud these two verses.

Then say: **In his letter to the church in Rome, Paul contrasts Adam and Christ. While Adam, through his sin, brought death to the human race, Christ, through one righteous act—dying for our sins—brought redemption and justification. And why did God give us this wonderful gift of salvation? Because God so loved the world that He gave His one and only Son, that whoever believes in Him should not perish but have eternal life** (John 3:16).

Facing the Music

(Needed: Paper, pencils)

Ask: **How often in the last week did you do something that your parent(s) specifically told you not to do?**

If your disobedience was found out, what, if any, punishment did you receive?

How did you feel when your sin was discovered? How do you think your parent(s) felt?

What, if any, mercy did you receive?

If your disobedience was not discovered, how do you feel about it now? How would your parent(s) feel if they knew you had deceived them? Get responses from several group members.

Then say: **Sometimes we feel great guilt when we're caught in the act by a person in authority over us. But when we think the person doesn't know about our wrongdoing, it's sometimes much easier to go on with our lives. Yet our conscience won't let us forget what we've done. In fact, it sometimes seems as if it's tormenting us until we admit our guilt. It's bad enough with our parents, because we know we must not only face the music if we admit disobedience, but we must also deal with our parents' disappointment. Let's think about how our disobedience impacts God.**

Distribute paper and pencils. Have group members write down their responses to the following questions:

How often in the last week did you do something that God has specifically commanded us not to do?

How do you think God feels about your sin?

What, if any, punishment do you think you should receive?

What feelings surface when you think about being caught in the act by God?

How do you feel about falling short of what God wants you to be?

Explain that it's difficult to feel accountable to a person we don't know or have contact with. Emphasize that in order to free ourselves from the feelings of shame over not measuring up to God's standards, to overcome the fear of death and punishment, to learn to live in a way that pleases God, we must grasp the gift of God's love—salvation through Jesus Christ. When we confess to God our shortcomings and ask His forgiveness, He will faithfully adopt us into His family by allowing His Spirit to live inside us.

If there are some kids in your group who have never received God's gift of salvation, now would be a good time to take them through the steps of salvation.

Say: **Let's take a few minutes to think and pray about the great plan God has provided for overcoming spiritual death and discovering a new way to live.**

First, let's use the list of our recent sins as a starting point for confession. Finish the following sentence in silent prayer: "God, here are some things I've done wrong this past week. In fact, there are some *other* things I've done that I probably ought to tell You about, including . . ." Allow several minutes for kids to pray.

Second, we need to ask God's forgiveness. You might say, "God, as I think about all of these sins in my life, I feel . . ." Allow several minutes for kids to tell God how they feel.

Third, we can now ask God to remove the judgment that we deserve for our sins because Jesus Christ has paid the price with His life. You might say, "God, thank You for sacrificing Your Son for me. I know I don't deserve to be free. When I think about what it cost Jesus to save me from death, I feel . . ." Encourage group members to personally commit themselves in faith to Christ as Savior. Allow several minutes for kids to thank God for Jesus' sacrifice.

Conclude by thanking God that His involvement in our lives is not limited to the past. Thank Him for sending Jesus to overcome the power of sin and make eternal life available to us. Thank Him for His continual involvement in our lives today through the Holy Spirit. Finally, praise Him for reestablishing personal contact with us, His most precious creation.

STEP 4

Our God Is Awesome

(Needed: Recording of and lyrics to Rich Mullins' song "Awesome God"; tape player)

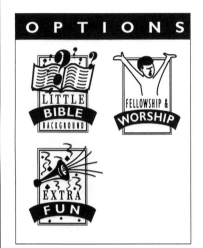

Before closing the session, suggest that anyone who established a personal relationship with God for the first time during this session contact you after the session. Also encourage those who may have reestablished contact with God to tell you so they can be prayed for during the week. Challenge anyone who still has questions about God's desire for a personal relationship with him or her to talk with you as soon as possible.

Distribute copies of the lyrics to Rich Mullins' song "Awesome God" (from the album, *Winds of Heaven, Stuff of Earth*). Play a recording of the song to give group members an idea of how it goes. Then sing the song as a group, affirming that God is powerful and loving enough to provide a plan of mercy and grace through the death of His Son.

IN THE BEGINNING... WHAT?   REPRO RESOURCE 6

What Would You Do?

Situation 1
You've been grounded (and that includes limited phone privileges) for getting a D in English and an F in History. Your mom and dad have left for an evening with friends. Before they left, they went over the rules, emphasizing no visits from friends or phone calls longer than five minutes. Ten minutes after your mom and dad leave, your best friend calls to tell you that a group of kids are on their way over to your house. You stay on the line, trying to figure out how the group knew your parents would be away. The doorbell rings and your little sister answers it. Six rowdy kids come bouncing in, heading for the refrigerator and the CD player. The group leaves three hours later. You decide to call your friend back with a full report of the evening. An hour later, the house is trashed and you're still on the phone when your mom and dad walk in, saying they've been trying to reach you for the last half hour. You respond by . . .

Situation 2
Your dad wants you to mow the lawn before you take off Saturday afternoon. You could finish in an hour if you used the riding lawnmower. But your dad says he doesn't want anyone to use the rider except himself. After sleeping late Saturday morning, you check the movie schedule. You see that if you use the push mower, you'll never make it to the movie in time. Your dad's gone to play golf, so he probably won't know the difference if you use the riding lawnmower. When you get home from the movie Saturday night, your dad is waiting for you—and he's angry. You discover that he decided to take the mower over to the church and it ran out of gas three blocks from home. You realize you forgot to gas up the rider when you finished using it. You respond by . . .

Situation 3
You come home from school starving. As you open the back door, the aroma of something fresh baked brings you to a standstill. There on the kitchen counter is a huge loaf of your mom's whole wheat bread. Next to the loaf is a note:

> Gone to the store. Don't touch—there's a box of raisins in the cupboard. See you in a while.
> Mom

You notice the loaf is still warm. The temptation is too great. As your mom comes in the door, you are spreading butter on your third fat slice. Your mom looks from you to the half loaf of bread and says, "I baked that especially for your brother at college. Now what can I send him?" You respond by . . .

IN THE BEGINNING... WHAT? REPRO RESOURCE 7

TRUTH and CONSEQUENCES

TEMPTATION Read Genesis 2:15-17; 3:1-7.

1. How would you describe the serpent in this passage? Do you think it's unusual that it *spoke* to Eve? (See Revelation 12:9.) What does the fact that the tempter appeared in the form of a snake suggest about temptation in general?

2. What was the element of truth in the serpent's question to Eve?

3. What restriction about the fruit did Eve add to God's command?

4. What did the serpent promise as a result of eating the fruit?

5. What did Eve and Adam hope to gain by eating the fruit?

6. What was the immediate consequence of disobeying God?

CONFRONTATION Read Genesis 3:8-13.

7. List a few words that describe Adam and Eve's first impulse upon hearing God in the garden. How does their reaction compare with your own when you're "caught in the act"?

8. God knew what Adam and Eve had done, yet how did He approach them? Does His gentle approach surprise you? Why or why not?

9. How did Adam try to shift responsibility for his disobedience? To whom do you try to shift responsibility for your own disobedience?

JUDGMENT Read Genesis 3:14-24.

10. Briefly describe the punishment set by God for

    • the serpent

    • Eve

    • Adam

11. Where in this passage do you find the first glimmer of the Gospel? Explain.

12. How did God express His grace to Adam and Eve after declaring His judgment?

13. Why did God banish Adam and Eve from the Garden?

OPTIONS

S E S S I O N   F O U R

Step 2
Have the "Temptation" team work in your meeting place, where you've planted a volunteer "tempter" who will try to get the team to ignore its assignment and opt for distractions you've left behind (refreshments, music, magazines, a game, etc.). Take the "Confrontation" and "Judgment" teams with you to study their passages in another spot. The Confrontation team, in addition to answering its questions, should plan to burst in on the Temptation team at your signal and confront it as God did Adam and Eve. The Judgment team should answer its questions and decide what punishment the Temptation team will receive if the latter didn't do its assignment (subject to your approval, of course). When the time comes, give your signal and see what happens. Then discuss what each team did and discovered.

Step 3
If you can meet outside, bring several sticks or spray cans of sidewalk chalk. Have kids form teams. Give chalk to each team. Instruct each team to color a two-foot-square (or larger) area of sidewalk or pavement to show what guilt "looks like." Have teams explain their drawings; then, as you describe how to become a Christian, wash the "guilt" away with a garden hose. If you have to stay inside, have each person take off one shoe and the corresponding sock. While the person has his or her eyes closed, place a small object (gummy worm, carrot stick, popcorn kernel, penny, etc.) in his or her shoe. Each person is to put his or her shoe back on, walk around for thirty seconds, and then guess what's in the shoe. Discuss how this experience is like living with guilt—walking around with something that bothers us, something we may not even be able to identify.

Step 2
Rather than having kids form teams to work through Repro Resource 7, a small group will probably do better to go through the sheet together. That way the questions that arise can be dealt with right away, and the group can move on together. It also removes pressure from group members who may not be as adept at working individually. However, be alert to anyone who tends to "fade out" during group activities. Make sure that everyone is involved in the discussion by asking pointed questions whenever you need to. (Asking opinion questions keeps kids involved without making them feel uncomfortable if they don't know the "right" answer.)

Step 3
As you discuss God's plan of salvation, try to make it very personal to your small group. Say: **When Jesus came to offer Himself as a sacrifice for the sins of the world, He could have made a big deal about it. But He didn't. What did He do? He assembled a small group to train and prepare to carry on when He was no longer physically present. His group members were a bunch of sinful, average people. Look around. We're a bunch of sinful, average people. What if we determined right now to learn as much as we can about Jesus and tried to carry on as if He were our leader—which, of course, He is?** Let kids begin to compare themselves to the original disciples. Help them see that God doesn't seek out privileged, overly intelligent, or exceptional people. He certainly doesn't exclude them, but He's eager to recruit *anyone* who is eager to get to know Him better. Jesus' first small group went on to accomplish great things. Your small group, provided with a little vision, can do the same.

Step 1
Begin the session with a game of "Caught in the Act." For this game, you'll need to block out as much light from your meeting area as possible. The darker your room is, the better the game will be. Give each person a nametag that he or she must wear on his or her back. The object of the game is simple—when you turn out the lights, group members must try to take each other's nametags without being caught. Periodically, you will turn on the lights. Anyone who is "caught in the act" of taking a nametag is out. Continue until only a few players are left. The person with the most nametags at the end is the winner. After the game, introduce the roleplays on Repro Resource 6.

Step 2
Instruct each of the three teams to present its findings in a creative manner. For instance, the "Temptation" team might present its information in the form of a TV commercial in which the serpent is a slick salesperson trying to "sell" Adam and Eve on the idea of eating the fruit by showing them all of the benefits they'll receive as a result. The "Confrontation" team might present its information in the form of a "60 Minutes"-like interview in which Adam and Eve are explaining their actions to an interviewer. The "Judgment" team might present its information in the form of a TV courtroom drama in which Adam, Eve, and the serpent receive the "sentences" for their sin.

OPTIONS

SESSION FOUR

Heard It All Before

Step 2
Kids may have heard the story of the Fall so many times that they've stopped listening. To get their attention, bring a live snake (if no one in your church has a pet snake, try buying a garter snake at a pet shop) and a piece of "exotic" fruit (pomegranate, mango, prickly pear, etc.). Have kids take a good look at the snake and pass around the fruit before even mentioning the passage you'll be studying. Then display the snake and the fruit as kids form study teams. Ask: **What's the most important part of the story about Adam and Eve's temptation—the snake or the fruit?** (Neither—the most important thing is what went on in the minds and hearts of Adam and Eve, the choice they made to disobey God.)

Step 3
If kids are likely to tune out the explanation of how to receive God's gift of salvation, prod them to come up with the explanation themselves. Have them form teams. Give each team three evangelistic tracts. The tracts should be widely varied in their approach—some old-fashioned, some contemporary, some funny, some somber. Each team must try to figure out how to become a Christian by finding what all of its tracts have in common. As teams share results, fill in gaps as needed.

Little Bible Background

Step 2
People with a good understanding of Scripture are accustomed to discussing issues such as temptation, confrontation, and judgment. However, these may be scary and delicate topics for your group members. That's no reason to avoid discussing them, of course, but you might want to follow up by discussing the New Testament issues of redemption, forgiveness, mercy, and grace. Have available a number of resource materials that will help you define and simplify these concepts. Make sure that no one is confused by the terminology. Assure kids that the truth of the Gospel story is quite simple, in spite of the many theological words that get attached. Be very open to any questions your kids might have.

Step 4
The opportunity is provided during this step for kids to make their first profession of faith. But in many cases, kids are likely to need a bit of prompting before they're comfortable doing so. For a group that is somewhat new to the Gospel, you might want to let kids write out any questions they have. A simple questionnaire can be nonthreatening. You might use questions such as the following:
• True or false: I understand everything that's been presented in this session.
• The questions I'm still struggling with are . . .
• True or false: I have made a personal commitment to God.
• The only thing(s) preventing me from making a commitment to God is/are . . .
• True or false: I think I would be able to explain the things in this session to someone else.

Fellowship & Worship

Step 2
Have your group members sit in a circle for a game of "hot potato." After you explain the rules of the game, start the potato hopping. Rather than using a real potato, however, find a plastic egg or some other hollow container into which you can stuff a prize for the "loser." (But don't tell the kids about it!) At the end of the game, have the loser open the "potato" to discover his or her prize. Explain: **Sin—and what we do with it—is like this game of "hot potato." Just as Adam and Eve did, we often try to pass the blame for our sin onto someone else and hope we don't get caught with it. But when we don't try to pass along our sin—when we bring it before God—we actually get the prize: forgiveness and salvation.**

Step 4
After your group members have listened to "Awesome God," have them continue their worship by writing a poem of praise to God for all of the examples they see of His awesome power—even in the seemingly small, everyday events of life. After a few minutes, ask volunteers to share their poems. Then close the session with prayer.

OPTIONS

SESSION FOUR

Mostly Girls

Step 1
Change Situation 2 on Repro Resource 6 as follows:
• You're babysitting for your new neighbors for the first time. They have a lot of expensive-looking crystal on display in a china cupboard. After you put the kids to bed, you decide to check it out. There's a small vase that you'd really like to see better. As you're taking it out of the case, you bump your arm and drop it. It's broken beyond repair; but you figure that the people have so many vases, they'll never miss it. You clean it all up and put it outside in the garbage can. Two days later, however, the neighbor comes over, asking if you remember seeing the vase. It was her great-grandmother's and was very special to her. You respond by . . .

Step 2
Hand out paper and pencils. Instruct group members to write across the top of their papers "The biggest temptation I struggle with right now is . . ." Give your girls a few minutes to fill in their responses. Afterward, ask volunteers to share what they wrote (but don't *force* anyone to share). Suggest that when we share our struggles, we can find help. Then pray for your girls and the struggles—spoken or unspoken—that each is facing.

Mostly Guys

Step 1
You may want to tailor some of the roleplays for your group of guys. In fact, you probably know of some of the specific things that your guys tend to struggle with. You can use these roleplays to see how they would respond in such situations. Some of the siutations that guys commonly face include the opportunity to drink at parties, being dared to steal something small from stores, the challenge to deface property or otherwise break the law, "stumbling upon" a friend's dad's *Hustler* magazine, and hearing locker-room talk about girls. Try to create roleplays that you know for sure your guys will relate to. (And if an actor does something out of character, the others should call him on it.)

Step 2
Whenever the fall of mankind is brought up, there is a widespread tendency among teenage guys to dodge all responsibility by shifting the blame to Eve and/or the entire female gender. As your guys read through the Genesis account and work through Repro Resource 7, direct their attention to Adam's willing participation in the event. Similarly, point out the tendency for some people to try to blame other people for all of their sins. Explain that the point of salvation is for us to be brutally honest about our own shortcomings and inadequacies. God will readily forgive us, but we miss out on His offer if we are trying too hard to save ourselves. Some guys don't like to be indebted to anyone. So when it comes to spiritual matters, they may need special attention before they are willing to yield to God.

Extra Fun

Step 1
Hand out pencils and paper. Instruct each person to write about a time when he or she was "caught in the act." The events group members describe should be fairly obscure so that not many people in the room will know which story is whose. The stories should also be written so as not to reveal the identity of the writer. (But emphasize that the stories *will* be read aloud and that the writer eventually will be identified.) After a few minutes, collect the sheets; read one at a time. After you read each story, let group members write down the name of the person that they think wrote it. After you've read all of the stories, let the writers identify themselves. As they do, have kids check their papers. Afterward, see who guessed the most correct names. Award prizes if you wish, but the fun of the activity is in learning other people's past secrets.

Step 4
Before you sing "Awesome God," pull out some songbooks and cut loose on some of your group members' other favorite songs. Challenge kids to select songs that reflect the reality of God's forgiveness and salvation. But rather than merely letting the lyrics roll by with little, if any, thought, have group members pay close attention to what they are singing. If kids can get excited about *what* they're singing rather than merely celebrating the opportunity to make noise together, they will have more fun than they've had in quite some time. And by the time you conclude with "Awesome God," the song should take on a new and deeper meaning for your kids.

OPTIONS

SESSION FOUR

Step 1
During the week before the session, use a VCR to record several TV commercials shown during children's cartoon shows. Try to include two toy commercials aimed at girls and two aimed at guys; a couple of ads for snack foods; and an ad for breakfast cereal. After showing the ads, ask: **How did these commercials try to "tempt" you to buy—or get your parents to buy—the products? Which did you think were most tempting and least tempting? Why? If you gave in to the "temptations," would you feel guilty? Why or why not? What kinds of real-life temptations, if you gave in to them, might make you feel guilty? Why?**

Step 3
Play one or more contemporary Christian songs that talk about guilt and forgiveness. After each song, ask: **How did this song leave you feeling? What does it say about the seriousness of doing something wrong? What does it say about God's willingness to forgive and how He does it?** Some examples of songs in this vein include "Brand New Start," "Old Man's Rubble," and "Open Arms" (Amy Grant); "Forgiven" (David Meece); "Love Found a Way" (Steve Green); "Man in the Middle" (Wayne Watson); and "Lamb of God" (Twila Paris).

Step 1
Try a shorter opener. Have two volunteers come to the front of the room and sit at a table. Tie a string to each volunteer's right wrist; hold the other end of each string. Explain that you're going to conduct a "lie detector test." You'll ask a question, and each volunteer will answer. If you sense "vibrations" from either person's hand, you'll know he or she is lying. Ask a question (place of birth, middle name, etc.). Accept the first person's answer as truthful, but as soon as the second one answers, jerk his or her string up and down. Mildly berate the second volunteer for "lying." Repeat the process with a different question, once again jerking the second person's string. Then do it again. Give the first volunteer a prize for "truthfulness" and the second a prize "to encourage you to tell the truth in the future." Ask the group: **Was that a fair test? Should** [name of second person] **feel guilty for "lying"? When should we feel guilty?** In Step 2, skip Repro Resource 7. Simply have teams read the passages and summarize for each other what happened. As needed, supplement with comments based on those in the session.

Step 3
Condense this step as follows. Ask: **When you do something wrong, who do you think feels worse about it—you or God? Why? What do you think God should do about your sins? What should you do about them?** Summarize how to receive God's gift of salvation. If time allows, let kids pray about any decisions they need to make in this area. If not, ask them to talk to you later about it. Skip Step 4.

Step 1
Replace Situation 2 on Repro Resource 6 with the following:
• One day, while you're hanging out on the street with your friends, a guy in a brand-new Mercedes pulls up and starts handing out all kinds of cool things, including tickets to the concert you've been dying to go to. Your mom has told you never to take things from strangers; but the guy in the Mercedes seems OK, so you accept the tickets. Later that night, your mom finds the tickets in your room and asks you where you got them. You respond by . . .

Step 3
Ask kids to share with the group the nicest thing that anyone has ever done for them or the greatest sacrifice that anyone has ever made for them. Compare your group members' stories with the sacrifice that Jesus made when He gave His life for us. To make the point a little more graphically, read the biblical account of Jesus' crucifixion in Luke 22:63–23:46. Afterward, discuss the role that Jesus' death and resurrection played in God's plan for humankind.

OPTIONS

SESSION FOUR

Step 1
Change the situations on Repro Resource 6 as follows:
- 1. When the friends come over, they show up with several six-packs and a few X-rated videos to "liven up the party."
- 2. You have a big date on Saturday night. You ask your dad if you can borrow the convertible—the car only he drives. He says no, but he's more than happy to let you take the family car. As you're heading out the door, you see his keys on the counter. He and your mom have friends visiting, so you know he won't miss the car. Off you go in the convertible. When you get home, however—with a scratch on the hood of the car—your dad is waiting. You respond by . . .

Step 2
Divide your group into two teams—a junior high team and a high school team. Distribute paper and pencils to each team. Instruct the members of each team to make a list of the typical temptations they face each day. After a few minutes, have each team share its list. As a group, discuss the fact that though the forms of temptation may change with our various ages and stages of life, the truth of temptation never changes. If temptation is not rejected, it leads to sin and separation from God. Fortunately, forgiveness and salvation are also available to all and never change.

Step 1
Rather than having your sixth graders roleplay the situations on Repro Resource 6, brainstorm as a group as many different responses (no matter how outrageous) as you can think of for each situation. After you've got a long list of responses for each situation, have your group members determine which response is best and explain why.

Step 3
It's possible that some of your sixth graders haven't had the Gospel message presented to them before. So you might want to take a few minutes to explain simply and clearly why Jesus came, what He did, what His sacrifice means for us, and how we can accept Him as Savior. Use passages like Romans 3:22-24; Romans 6:23; and I John 1:9 in your presentation. Allow plenty of time for questions and discussion.

Date Used:

Approx. Time

Step 1: Choose Your Own Endings ____
- o Large Group
- o Mostly Girls
- o Mostly Guys
- o Extra Fun
- o Media
- o Short Meeting Time
- o Urban
- o Combined Junior High/High School
- o Sixth Grade

Things needed:

Step 2: Not Off to a Very Good Start ____
- o Extra Action
- o Small Group
- o Large Group
- o Heard It All Before
- o Little Bible Background
- o Fellowship & Worship
- o Mostly Girls
- o Mostly Guys
- o Combined Junior High/High School

Things needed:

Step 3: Facing the Music ____
- o Extra Action
- o Small Group
- o Heard It All Before
- o Media
- o Short Meeting Time
- o Urban
- o Sixth Grade

Things needed:

Step 4: Our God Is Awesome ____
- o Little Bible Background
- o Fellowship & Worship
- o Extra Fun

Things needed:

SESSION 5
The New Creation

YOUR GOALS FOR THIS SESSION:
Choose one or more

☐ To help kids see that to be in Christ is to be a new creation.

☐ To help kids understand that their new life in Christ means that God is developing in them new attitudes and actions.

☐ To help kids begin to look to the future, when God's new creative work will be completed.

☐ Other _____

Your Bible Base:

II Corinthians 5:17
Ephesians 4:22, 24-32
Revelation 21:1-7;
  22:1-5

OPTIONS

STEP 1

Give Me a New Look

(Needed: Make-up supplies, prizes)

As much as possible, have your group members form guy-girl pairs. Hand out make-up supplies to each pair. Instruct the girls to do make-overs on the guys, trying to create a new look for them. After a few minutes (and a lot of complaining from the guys), award a prize for the best make-over. Then turn the tables and allow the guys to make over the girls. After a few minutes, award a prize for the best make-over. Afterward, explain that when God does "make-overs" on us, He starts His work from the *inside*.

STEP 2

Eternal Make-overs

(Needed: Bibles, copies of Repro Resource 8, pencils, poster)

Have someone read aloud II Corinthians 5:17. Then ask: **What does it mean to be a new creation? How is it brought about?**

If no one mentions it, explain: **To "be in Christ" refers to our spiritual relationship to Christ. When we believe the message of the Gospel—that Jesus died for our sins on the cross and was resurrected—our reconciliation to God is made possible. This new creation is brought about by the indwelling of the Holy Spirit. We find new life as we seek and depend on the Holy Spirit's guidance to break with our past ways.**

However, letting go of the old ways is easier said than done. In Ephesians 4, the apostle Paul encouraged Christians to "put off" the old self (4:22). **In other words, we must stop living the "have-it-our-way" life that never provides true joy and satisfaction. Rather, we are to "put on the new self"**

(4:24). **In the rest of Ephesians 4, Paul shows us five evidences of the Holy Spirit's creative work in our lives.**

Divide the group into study teams to discuss and report on Paul's list of new ways of being and acting. Distribute copies of "What's Wrong with This Picture?" (Repro Resource 8) and pencils. Instruct the teams to identify a negative and positive instruction from each verse or passage. The teams should also write down a reason for the positive instruction. After several minutes, reassemble the group and discuss. As kids work through the passage, encourage them to consider one area of their lives in which they have recently struggled in terms of living for themselves rather than for Christ. Use the following information to supplement your discussion of the passages.

Ephesians 4:25

We are instructed to tell the truth and not lie, because we are all members of Christ's body, the church.

Ask: **What difference does it make to Christ whether we lie or not? What difference does it make to the church? To others in this group?** Get several responses.

Ephesians 4:26, 27

We are instructed to be angry and deal with our anger—and not to let our anger control us. By keeping short accounts (dealing with anger before "the sun [goes] down"), we can prevent anger from getting a foothold and leading us into sin.

Say: **Give an example of a time when you were angry and you managed your anger fairly well. Then share a time when your anger kept festering until it controlled you. Why do you think anger is sometimes a hard feeling to deal with properly?**

Ephesians 4:28

We are instructed to work and earn the material things we need rather than steal from others. Believers are to work so that they can share with others who are in need.

Ask: **When was the last time someone shared something with you? When was the last time you shared something with another person? What keeps you from sharing more with others?**

Ephesians 4:29, 30

We are instructed to verbally build others up, not tear them down. If what we say doesn't benefit or edify the person, the Holy Spirit is grieved. In addition, sometimes the person is grieved.

Ask: **When you think of someone who verbally builds you up, what person comes to mind? Do you think your name comes to mind when others think about someone who builds them up? Why or why not?**

Ephesians 4:31, 32

Paul summarizes what happens when we give in to the old self—lying,

raging, stealing, slandering, and being wicked. We are instructed to be kind, compassionate, and forgiving, because this is what we have experienced from God because of Christ's sacrifice.

Ask: **Which of the following things do you struggle with most—lying, bitterness, uncontrollable anger, stealing, or verbal abuse of others? Explain. What needs to take place in order for us to want to be truthful, to deal with anger in a healthy way, to be kind, compassionate, forgiving, verbally affirming, etc?**

Before the session, you'll need to create a poster with the following information on it. Display the poster at this point in the session.

"We welcome the Holy Spirit's work in our lives by asking Him to
• Give us a desire to experience unity with other believers;
• Help us understand that bitterness and rage have negative, undesirable consequences for us and for those at whom we direct them;
• Soften our hearts toward looking beyond our own needs and sharing with others;
• Make us aware of the power of our words;
• Remind us of the compassion, forgiveness, and grace God offers us through His Son."

Discuss as a group what kind of inner work the Holy Spirit is doing in order for us to *act* like new creatures. Explain that all of these changes in the way we think and feel can be transformed inwardly so that genuine acts of truthfulness, self-control, kindness, forgiveness, affirmation, etc. can be evident on the outside. As we seek to obey God, it is really the Holy Spirit who is working in us.

Ask: **What happens when we try to change our actions without changing the way we feel inside?** Get several responses.

Face to Face

(Needed: Bibles)

Say: **God's new creative work, begun in each of us who believes in Christ, will one day be completed and perfect. Let's take a look at the future.**

Read aloud Revelation 21:1-7 and 22:1-5. Explain that the Book of Revelation is the last book of the Bible. The book is filled with end-time events, but the last two chapters of Revelation describe the creation of a new heaven, a new earth, and a new Jerusalem. While we could spend a lot of time exploring the many interpretations of the end-time events, we want to focus on how God will relate to His adopted children when He completes His creative work.

Ask: **How does the fact that God will dwell with us differ from the indwelling of His Holy Spirit** (Revelation 21:3)? If no one suggests it, explain that in eternity, we will enjoy a new intimacy with God—perhaps the kind of intimacy that Adam and Eve experienced in the Garden of Eden prior to their sin or even greater.

How do you feel about the idea of no more death, sorrow, or pain? Explain that God's sentence of pain and struggle, death, and separation for Eve and Adam will be no more. In contrast to banishment from the garden to prevent Adam and Even from eating from the tree of life, God offers water of life or spiritual blessings to all who are thirsty. He offers the full intimacy of parenthood and leaves for healing. Finally, God tells us that in eternity there will be no curse. Notice in Revelation 22:5 that in the new creation, we will need no solar sources for heat or light; God's presence will be sufficient. But most importantly, we will see His face (22:4).

Ask: **How do you feel about the prospect of seeing God face to face? Why?** Get several responses.

What's New?

(Needed: Recording of Leslie Phillip's song "By My Spirit," tape player)

Ask: **After examining what it means to be a new creation of God, what areas in your life still need work or seem to be under construction?** Get a few responses.

Then play a recording of "By My Spirit" by Leslie Phillips (from the album *Dancing with Danger*). Have your kids focus on one area of their lives in which they need to seek the Holy Spirit's guidance. Remind them of the ways that the Holy Spirit works in our lives:
 • He gives us a desire to experience unity with other believers;
 • He helps us understand that bitterness and rage have negative, undesirable consequences for us and those at which we direct them;
 • He softens our hearts toward looking beyond our own needs and sharing with others;
 • He makes us aware of the power of our words;

• He reminds us of the compassion, forgiveness, and grace God offers us through His Son.

At the conclusion of the song, suggest that each person share one way he or she would like to be transformed or changed from the inside out.

Explain: **Sharing with the group how you would like to be transformed is a risk because it will bring accountability. For example, if I want to be more aware of the power of my words, others in the room have the responsibility of letting me know when I hurt them *or* affirm them. So, don't share how you want to be changed if you don't mean it. Remember, the Holy Spirit is working inside to change your attitudes and the thoughts behind your words.**

After a time of sharing, close the session by asking God to help your group members experience and express more of His compassion, forgiveness, and grace with each other.

IN THE BEGINNING... WHAT?

REPRO RESOURCE 8

What's Wrong with This Picture?

	+ Dos	**−** Don'ts	**?** Whys
Ephesians 4:25			
Ephesians 4:26, 27			
Ephesians 4:28			
Ephesians 4:29, 30			
Ephesians 4:31, 32			

OPTIONS

SESSION FIVE

Extra Action

Step 2
Instead of handing out Repro Resource 8, cut the five references and the five pictures from the sheet so that you end up with five separate slips with references on them and five separate pictures. If you have more than five group members, make and cut more copies of the sheet so that each person can have a reference slip and a picture. Give each person a reference slip and a picture that doesn't match that reference. Explain that the actions in each picture show the *opposite* of the instructions in one of the references. Have kids look up their references. Then kids should mill around, with each person acting out his or her picture (expletive-shouters should stick with "blankety-blank") and trying to find someone whose reference relates to his or her picture. When a match is found, partners should briefly discuss what the passage says about how "new creatures" are to act. Continue the process until everyone has found matches for his or her picture and reference.

Step 3
Bring a roll of waxed paper and some masking tape. After briefly discussing the Revelation passages, put half of the group on one side of a doorway and half on the other side. Tape pieces of waxed paper over the doorway until the doorway is covered. At your signal, one person from each side of the doorway will step up to the paper and try to guess the identity of the person on the other side. Kids probably will find that they must get nose-to-nose before they can identify each other. If you wish, give a prize to each one who correctly identifies the other person. Then read I Corinthians 13:9-12. Ask: **What do you hope becomes clear to you in heaven?** After hearing replies, let kids break through the waxed-paper wall to see each other face to face.

Small Group

Step 1
If you really want to give members of your small group something to remember, let them work together to give *you* a makeover. Be sure to take "before" and "after" pictures for posterity. Not only will this give your young people a cherished memory and a lot of laughs, but it will also make your introduction to the session even more effective. As you are scraping off the cherry red lipstick and blue eye shadow, you can point out that this is about the best we can expect if we try to improve ourselves without God's help. Then you can move on to Step 2 to discuss what God can do to make us over without making us look ridiculous.

Step 2
Let individuals (rather than groups) be responsible for each of the sections of Repro Resource 8. But explain that you want to reward deep thinking as people work on their own. Offer pieces of wrapped candy or similar rewards for every question people can ask (based on the biblical material covered) that no one else can answer. In most cases, group members will actually be asking what they themselves don't understand, so you can deal with real and valid questions. You will also be able to see rather quickly how well people comprehend the material by using the question-and-answer approach.

Large Group

Step 1
If your group is really large, you might have difficulty finding enough makeup to supply several guy-girl pairs. So instead, try a variation of the activity. Bring in enough makeup—and costumes—for three people. The more elaborate and outrageous the costumes, the more fun this activity will be. Have kids form three teams. Give each team a set of makeup and a costume. Have each team select a member to be "made over." That person must cooperate while the rest of the team dresses and puts makeup on him or her. Give the teams about ten minutes to work. When they're finished, stage a "beauty contest" to determine which team did the best job with its make-over. Afterward, point out that when God does "makeovers," He works from the inside.

Step 4
Some of your group members may feel uncomfortable about sharing with a large group of people. To address this problem, have kids form groups of four. Encourage each person to share with the others in his or her small group one way in which he or she would like to be transformed or changed from the inside out. After everyone has had an opportunity to share, have the members of each small group pray together for each other's needs. Suggest that the members of each small group stay in contact with each other during the week, offering each other support and encouragement.

O P T I O N S

S E S S I O N   F I V E

HEARD IT ALL BEFORE

Step 2
Kids may like the Step 1 idea of a "make-over" that makes them more attractive, but may tune you out when you describe a "make-over" that would force them to follow a bunch of rules. As you discuss the Ephesians passages, help kids see how putting off the "old self" and becoming a new creation could make them more "attractive" to others as well as to God. For example, do most kids want to be friends with liars or truth-tellers? Do kids want to spend time with those who "blow up" when angry? Which is more appealing, someone who's always "mooching" or someone who shares? Do kids like friends who build them up or tear them down?

Step 3
Kids may have heard many times that heaven involves an *absence* of certain things—pain, tears, death, etc. But what's left? Harps? Shuffleboard? To get kids thinking about what the curse-lifting could mean, have teams brainstorm what the following activities might be like if there were no such thing as pain, no limits placed on us by earthly bodies, and plenty of time to practice: football, bungee jumping, basketball, pole vaulting. Explain that we don't know whether we'll do these things in heaven; the point is that the *subtraction* of negative things in God's new creation will make possible the *addition* of positive things we can't even imagine.

LITTLE BIBLE BACKGROUND

Step 2
If your kids aren't familiar with the Bible, don't divide into groups to work on Repro Resource 8. Questions are likely to arise all the way through, and if you're all working on the sheet together you will save time in the long run by discussing questions as they come up. It should also be encouraging for your kids to learn to interact with each other as they deal with Bible passages. Be prepared to help your kids understand the nature and work of the Holy Spirit. Even people who grow up in the church frequently find it difficult to comprehend God being within us, working through our conscience, directing our emotions, and so forth. Take your time as you help people who are new to the Bible understand these truths. (You might also want to have some good resources for kids to take home and peruse on their own.)

Step 3
The Revelation account of life in the presence of God is likely to be new to many young people who don't know much about the Bible. They may have a natural curiosity about what you believe will happen in the future. Be prepared to spend some time addressing their questions. Since you've been dealing with the Genesis account, explain that you're simply zipping ahead to the end of the story for anyone who seeks out the relationship with God that Adam and Eve damaged, but that Jesus restored. At this early point in their interest in Scripture, you probably want to keep their focus on Revelation to the last two chapters. Later, after they learn more about Old Testament symbolism and the life of Jesus, perhaps they will be ready to try to take on more of John's prophetic book.

FELLOWSHIP & WORSHIP

Step 1
Before the session gets rolling, take your kids outside for a quick game (a good team fellowship builder). If weather prohibits and your facility permits, you might clear some space in your meeting area for your kids to play, using a foam rubber soccer ball. After the game, say: **While God makes us into a new creation on the inside, we need to remember to take care of ourselves on the outside. Exercise and having fun are important parts of living balanced, God-honoring lives.**

Step 3
Set up tables with creative (but inexpensive) arts and crafts supplies. Have kids refer back to Revelation 21:1-7 and 22:1-5. Instruct group members to pick out one description of heaven from the passage and create something that is a representation of that description. Kids may draw, paint, sculpt, write a poem—anything that is an expression of something about heaven that excites them. (You may wish to emphasize that it doesn't need to be a literal interpretation or representation.) When everyone is finished, ask volunteers to share and explain their work. Then have kids pray silently, thanking God for the gift He offers us in heaven.

OPTIONS

SESSION FIVE

Mostly Girls

Step 1
Girls, especially junior high girls, love make-up and doing make-overs. If there are no guys in your group—or too few to pair with the girls—pair the girls with each other. However, give them a "theme" for their make-overs—the most creative use of color, the most intimidating look, or something similar. Award prizes to the pair that best expresses the theme.

Step 2
If you have a kitchen available, take your girls there. Divide them into two baking teams. Give each team a recipe for cookies or some other goodies that are made from scratch. Provide ingredients for the teams and let them go about their baking. However, quietly instruct one team to use salt rather than sugar in their cookies. Later in the session, when the cookies are done, let your girls taste the fruit of their labor. When some of the girls complain about the taste of some of the cookies, explain what you did. Then say: **Just as these cookies looked good from the outside, there are people who may look good on the outside but are really rotten inside. We can make ourselves look good through our actions, but if we don't have the right ingredients working in us— God, Jesus, the Holy Spirit—we won't "taste" any better than these horrible cookies.**

Mostly Guys

Step 1
Rather than have your guys give each other make-overs, bring a number of magazines to the meeting instead. Be sure to include a number of sports and fitness magazines. Ask kids to thumb through the magazines until they find a photo that indicates what they would like to look like if they could. Let everyone show the picture he chooses to the rest of the group. Then ask: **What are you doing to become more like the person in the photo you chose? Do you think God is doing anything to help you become that person?** Help your guys see that it's more important to try to become the person God wants us to be rather than who we might want to be. While God certainly provides life, health, and strength to get in better shape and build ourselves physically, His primary desire is that we attend to our *spiritual* fitness.

Step 4
Many guys will probably need a bit of prompting for this activity—first to admit that they might *need* to change for the better, and then to agree to be held accountable. They may need more of an extrinsic incentive to motivate them. At the end of this step, after you've challenged them to share something they wish to change about themselves and be held accountable for, place a jar at the front of the room. Ask all group members to be on the alert to help each other make the changes they've shared. Each time someone witnesses a behavior one of the guys has said he wants to get rid of, he should tell the guy about it and "fine" him 25¢ for the violation. Collect the money in the jar over a period of time. Later, use it to go out and do something fun, recalling the mistakes that made the celebration possible and acknowledging the spiritual growth that is beginning to take place within the group.

Extra Fun

Step 1
Play a quick drawing game similar to Pictionary, but using words associated with "new." But don't let kids know until afterward what the common theme is. Words you might use include *deal, republic, year, born, found, Jersey, Mexico, moon, world, wave, testament,* and so forth. After several rounds, conclude with the word *you*. See if anyone can identify the unifying theme for all of the words that were used. Then move on to the make-over activity.

Step 3
After you go through the discussion of Revelation, but before you ask the final question in this step, hand out markers and drawing paper. Ask group members to create an artistic masterpiece entitled "The Best Thing about Heaven." After a few minutes, let everyone display and explain his or her picture. See if the focus of group members' pictures is on the presence of God or on their own "benefits." While the two things are closely connected, challenge kids to dwell on what it means to be in the presence of God without fear of correction or reproach. If possible, display the pictures somewhere around the church where other people can see them.

OPTIONS

SESSION FIVE

Step 1
Show the following scenes (after pre-screening for appropriateness) from one or more of these videos:
• *Teen Wolf; Teen Wolf Too;* or *I Was a Teenage Werewolf.* Show a scene in which a teenager is transformed into a werewolf. Ask: **Do you ever feel like you're undergoing this kind of change? If you could change into a "new creature," what kind would you want it to be?**
• *Terminator 2: Judgment Day.* Play a scene in which the T-1000 cyborg, made of liquid metal, "morphs" from his human shape into something else. Ask: **Have you ever wished you could change into something or someone else? If so, what or who would that something or someone be?**
• *Star Trek: The Motion Picture.* Show the scene near the end in which a man and woman are transformed by an alien power into glowing, "advanced" beings. Ask: **If you could change into a "new creature," would it be a creature like this? Why or why not?**

Step 2
At the start of the step, play a few songs that seem based on the values of "the old self" (listen yourself beforehand for appropriateness). Each time you read a Bible verse during this step, discuss which songs might need to be rewritten to reflect the values of the "new creation" mentioned in that verse. At the end of the step, skip the poster and have kids rewrite at least part of one song in a way that sums up your discussion. Some "old self" songs might include "Crazy for You" (Madonna), "Money for Nothing" (Dire Straits), "What's Love Got to Do with It" (Tina Turner), "We're Not Gonna Take It" (Twisted Sister), and "Saturday Night's Alright for Fighting" (Elton John).

Step 1
Try a shorter opener. Write the following on the board: "Youth Group Car Wash"; "Ice Cream Social"; "Summer Beach Party"; "Road Rally." Say: **Here are some youth group events. By adding, subtracting, or replacing just one letter in the name of each event, you can come up with a totally new and strange event. Do that in one minute, and you'll win a prize. Your changed words must be real words. Go!** After a minute, see what kids have come up with. More than one answer may be possible, but here are some suggestions: "Youth Group Carp Wash"; "Lice Cream Social"; "Summer Bach Party"; "Toad Rally." Use this activity to introduce the idea that even small changes can lead to the creation of something new. Replace Step 2 with a discussion of II Corinthians 5:17; Galatians 5:19-26; and Philippians 1:6. Ask: **What does each passage say about what God wants to do with us? How do you feel about that?** As needed, explain that growing the "fruit" of the Spirit takes time; our job is to be willing to let God change us.

Step 3
Replace Steps 3 and 4 with the following. Read Revelation 21:1-5. Have kids form pairs. Explain that you'll name a kind of relationship; then, when you say "Old," partners should strike a pose showing a conflict that two people with that relationship might have with each other in this life. When you say "New," they should pose to show how the same two people might relate in heaven. Here are some categories: boss and worker; parent and teenager; teacher and student; youth leader and group member; two candidates for a student office; boyfriend and girlfriend. Then ask: **Why did you pose as you did? What changes might God have to make in you before your relationships are "heavenly"?** Have kids pray silently about those changes.

Step 1
Give your kids an opportunity to do a fictional "make-over" on the neighborhood or area in which they live. Ask: **If you could clean up or change the area where you live, or do anything else you wanted to make your neighborhood better, what would you do?** Encourage kids to use their creativity as they respond to this question. As kids share their ideas, pay attention to which suggestions are "cosmetic" (concerned with surface appearance) and which are more substantial. Afterward, point out that when God does "make-overs" on people, He starts His work from the *inside*.

Step 2
Ask volunteers to talk about people they know (without using names) whose lives and personalities have been completely changed due to alcohol or drug abuse. You should be prepared to share a few examples of your own. Compare those negative changes with the wonderful changes that occur in a person's life when he or she becomes a new creation in Christ.

OPTIONS

SESSION FIVE

Step 1
Rather than having your group members form guy-girl pairs, have them form junior high-high school pairs. Give your junior highers an opportunity to do make-overs on the high schoolers. Award prizes to the best junior-high make-over artist and the strangest-looking made-over high schooler. Afterward, emphasize that God works on the *inside*, despite how much we focus on the outside.

Step 2
After discussing the poster of the Holy Spirit's work in our lives, give each group member a piece of paper and a pencil. Challenge kids to work down the list of items on the poster one by one, writing down specifically what each point means in their own lives. Say: **It's much easier to talk about change like this as a group, to keep it all theoretical, to look at what the other guy needs to do. It's a lot more difficult to turn that kind of scrutiny inward and do something about it.** Challenge kids to work on their lists, to really open themselves to the touch of the Holy Spirit.

Step 1
If you're a little wary of letting your sixth graders play with makeup, try another option. Bring in several Halloween masks. One at a time, have group members come to the front of the room. Hand each person a mask. When the person puts on the mask, he or she should act accordingly. For instance, someone with a cowboy mask should act like a cowboy; someone with a monster mask should act like a monster; etc. After you've had some fun with this activity, point out that the "changes" in your group members were superficial—they were the result of wearing a mask. On the other hand, when God changes us, He works from the *inside*.

Step 2
To illustrate the idea of putting off the old self (Ephesians 4:22), bring in pictures of a snake that has shed its skin. (Of course, it would be way cool if you could bring in an actual snake with its actual shed skin; however, if you're reptilianally challenged, pictures will suffice.) Ask: **What are some of the things that we "put off" when we become new creatures in Christ?**

Date Used:

Approx. Time

Step 1: Give Me a New Look   _____
o Small Group
o Large Group
o Fellowship & Worship
o Mostly Girls
o Mostly Guys
o Extra Fun
o Media
o Short Meeting Time
o Urban
o Combined Junior High/High School
o Sixth Grade
Things needed:

Step 2: Eternal Make-overs   _____
o Extra Action
o Small Group
o Heard It All Before
o Little Bible Background
o Mostly Girls
o Media
o Urban
o Combined Junior High/High School
o Sixth Grade
Things needed:

Step 3: Face to Face   _____
o Extra Action
o Heard It All Before
o Little Bible Background
o Fellowship & Worship
o Extra Fun
o Short Meeting Time
Things needed:

Step 4: What's New?   _____
o Large Group
o Mostly Guys
Things needed:

Custom Curriculum Critique

Please take a moment to fill out this evaluation form, rip it out, fold it, tape it, and send it back to us. This will help us continue to customize products for you. Thanks!

1. Overall, please give this *Custom Curriculum* course (*In the Beginning . . . What?*) a grade in terms of how well it worked for you. (A=excellent; B=above average; C=average; D=below average; F=failure) Circle one.

   A   B   C   D   F

2. Now assign a grade to each part of this curriculum that you used.

a. Upfront article	A	B	C	D	F	Didn't use
b. Publicity/Clip art	A	B	C	D	F	Didn't use
c. Repro Resource Sheets	A	B	C	D	F	Didn't use
d. Session 1	A	B	C	D	F	Didn't use
e. Session 2	A	B	C	D	F	Didn't use
f. Session 3	A	B	C	D	F	Didn't use
g. Session 4	A	B	C	D	F	Didn't use
h. Session 5	A	B	C	D	F	Didn't use

3. How helpful were the options?
   - ❏ Very helpful
   - ❏ Somewhat helpful
   - ❏ Not too helpful
   - ❏ Not at all helpful

4. Rate the amount of options:
   - ❏ Too many
   - ❏ About the right amount
   - ❏ Too few

5. Tell us how often you used each type of option (4=Always; 3=Sometimes; 2=Seldom; 1=Never)

	4	3	2	1
Extra Action	❏	❏	❏	❏
Combined Jr. High/High School	❏	❏	❏	❏
Urban	❏	❏	❏	❏
Small Group	❏	❏	❏	❏
Large Group	❏	❏	❏	❏
Extra Fun	❏	❏	❏	❏
Heard It All Before	❏	❏	❏	❏
Little Bible Background	❏	❏	❏	❏
Short Meeting Time	❏	❏	❏	❏
Fellowship and Worship	❏	❏	❏	❏
Mostly Guys	❏	❏	❏	❏
Mostly Girls	❏	❏	❏	❏
Media	❏	❏	❏	❏
Extra Challenge (High School only)	❏	❏	❏	❏
Sixth Grade (Jr. High only)	❏	❏	❏	❏

(tape here)

BUSINESS REPLY MAIL
FIRST CLASS MAIL   PERMIT NO 1   ELGIN IL

POSTAGE WILL BE PAID BY ADDRESSEE

Attn: Youth Department
David C Cook Publishing Co
850 N GROVE AVE
ELGIN IL 60120-9980

NO POSTAGE
NECESSARY
IF MAILED
IN THE
UNITED STATES

---

6. What did you like best about this course?

7. What suggestions do you have for improving *Custom Curriculum*?

8. Other topics you'd like to see covered in this series:

9. Are you?
   ❑ Full time paid youthworker
   ❑ Part time paid youthworker
   ❑ Volunteer youthworker

10. When did you use *Custom Curriculum*?
    ❑ Sunday School   ❑ Small Group
    ❑ Youth Group   ❑ Retreat
    ❑ Other _____

---

11. What grades did you use it with? _____

12. How many kids used the curriculum in an average week? _____

13. What's the approximate attendance of your entire Sunday school program (Nursery through Adult)? _____

14. If you would like information on other *Custom Curriculum* courses, or other youth products from David C. Cook, please fill out the following:

    Name: _____
    Church Name: _____
    Address: _____
    _____
    Phone: (____) _____

    Thank you!